AIR BRIDGE 2

The design, development and service use of the ATL98 Carvair conversions

and their effect on the civilian vehicle air ferry era

Paul A. Doyle

Forward Airfield Research Publishing》》

First published in 2000 by
Forward Airfield Research Publishing
14 Clydesdale Road
Royston, Hertfordshire SG8 9JA

ISBN 0 9525624 7 2

Typesetting by
West 4 Printers Ltd 8 Essex Place, London W4 5UT

Printed and bound in England by
Woolnough Bookbinding Ltd.
Express Works, Church Street
Irthlingborough, Northants NN9 5SE

By the same author/publisher

Where the Lysanders were . . . (the story of Sawbridgeworth's airfields)
Fields of the First – A history of aircraft landing grounds in Essex used during the First World War

Front cover photograph:

Passengers, cars and freight – the Carvair could swallow them all, easily. Atmospheric shot of a typical vehicle-ferry operation, in this case the turn-round of two British Air Ferries Carvairs G-APNH, 'Menai Bridge' (front) and G-ASDC, 'Pont du Rhin', positioned to Lydd from Southend in October 1968. *(Ken Bailey photo)*

Contents

Acknowledgements

Between 1974-77 many people, primarily ex-vehicle ferry operatives, were contacted about the cross-channel era. Every contact made resulted in us being welcomed into their homes or offices, which in so doing took up much of their valuable time. To all those who helped in our researches, especially those persons still in the aircraft industry at the time we dealt with them, by memory-jogging or the supply of information and photographs so that this story could be told, our grateful thanks are extended.

Principal thanks to:

Air Transport Division, Canada
Ken Bailey, Maintenance Engineer, Lydd Airport (Silver City Airways)
Debbie Ball and Nanette Smith, Brandon, Suffolk
Len Birch, Lydd Airport (SCA)
Cliff Bishop, Design Liaison Engineer, Stansted (Aviation Traders Engineering Ltd)
British Rail Shipping & International Services Division
Don B. Cartlidge, Carvair programme chief test pilot (ATEL)
Ken Cole (British Air Ferries)
Robert D. Comer, ITT Federal Services, RAF Mildenhall
Tony E.H. Cotgrove (ex-ATEL)
Guy Craven (BAF)
Department of Transport, Australia
Department of Transport and Power, Eire
the late John DeWoolfson, Commandant, Lydd Airport (SCA)
Dominica de Aviacion, Dominicana
Christopher and Kirsten Doyle
Freddie Foster (SCA & BAF)
the French Embassy, London
Robert C.S. Graham (Eastern Provincial Airways, Canada)
André Van Gyseghem, Assistant Manager, Ostende Airport
the late James Halley
Norris Heritage, Lydd Airport (SCA/Hurds)
Historic Aircraft Museum, Southend
Harry Holmes, Manchester
Maurice Jeffrey (BAF)
Jimmy Jones (BAF)
Brian Kerry, Chief Aerodynamicist (ATEL)
Sir Freddie Laker (ex-Bond Air Services & British United Air Ferries)
the late Bob Langley DFC, Carvair programme deputy test pilot, Chief Pilot Channel Air Bridge
Arthur C. Leftley, Chief Design Engineer (ATEL)
Terry Leighton (ATEL), FLS Aerospace (UK) Ltd, Stansted Airport
Janice Mason, Unisys, Milton Keynes
Ministère Des Transports, Grand Duchy of Luxembourg
National Ports Council, London
Tony Oliver (BAF)
Philip Pegg, Civil Airworthiness Authority, Southend
David M. Pugh, (fellow instigator of this work) Southend
Terry Roper, Loftsman (ATEL)
Gerry Rosser, Captain (SCA)
Jack Lawrence Rowe, Captain (BAF)
Secretary of Civil Aviation, Spain
Secrétariat D'etat Aux Transports, France
Ken Smith, Flight Test Engineer, Carvair programme (ATEL)
Bill Souter (BAF)
Tony Underhill (BAF)
United Nations Archives, New York
the late Dick Worthington (BAF)

Introduction

In 1974, as the Carvair was coming to the end of its UK vehicle ferry life, a colleague and I toyed with the idea of writing a history of the use of this aircraft on the cross-Channel vehicle ferry routes. For more than three years we then toured both this country and the channel coast of Europe to meet people who had been concerned with the vehicle ferry, and corresponded with overseas operators, but after a short while were of the opinion that the concept leading up to what became the Carvair had started some 25 years before, and then subsequently became a world-wide operation, not confined solely to Europe.

When research started the main intention was purely to relate the day-to-day workings of the Carvair in use from 1962 with British and French operators on the short-haul, cross-Channel routes. However it was found necessary to dig deeper into the past and record not only the development and history of all the aircraft considered and/or used from the time of the 're-birth' of civil airlines after the dark days of the Second World War but also the history of these companies.

This volume deals entirely and concisely with the inception and service use of the ATL98 Carvair, as the logical replacement for the earlier Bristol Freighter vehicle ferry types, and gives an outline of the working practices employed by all the companies who used the type from 1962 to 1975. The earlier vehicle-ferry period, 1945 to 1962, will be covered in a separate volume, and my only regret is that it has taken so long to commit it to print.

Paul A Doyle
Royston, Herts, 2000

To the pioneers in the British aircraft industry

With the aircraft on Stand 2 and the freight handlers on Stand 3, six yacht masts 54' 0" in length are loaded into Carvair G-APNH at Southend. As can be seen, the operation took up a lot of ramp space and the well-used Hylo had to be supplemented with manpower during this type of exercise – or should the words 'balancing act' be used!

(BAF photo)

The design stage

The Bristol Type 170, conceived in 1945 as a rugged freighter for the Royal Air Force and designed to cope with rough, unimproved jungle airstrips in the Far East, had carried out sterling work on the Berlin Airlift before being pressed into service with the civilian air transport operators that emerged after the Second World War. Having never been adopted by the British air forces it was left to the private companies to make use of it, and this they did on the short cross-Channel routes set up from airfields in southern England to those on the near coast of Continental Europe. The original design, known as the Mk 21, had a 'solid' nose but the Mk 31 Freighter had clam-shell nose doors which afforded easier loading, and allowed what was then a fairly useful load of three cars and their passengers to be carried. Under these loading conditions only short stage lengths could be operated, but this was not critical in the early days of this embryo service.

In an attempt to broaden the market for the Freighter the Bristol Aeroplane Company did a re-work on the basic design by extending the nose length, such that a further car could be carried. In stretching the basic Bristol design to the Mark 32, or 'Superfreighter', the carriage of freight was improved but the fact still remained that whilst the new type was now able to carry four cars, and a further four passengers than the Mark 31, it was still limited in stage length to destinations in Northern Europe under these loading conditions and only able to extend its range if an intermediate refuelling stop was made en route. A further nail in its coffin for the type was the limitation placed on the life of the wing spar as a result of stresses produced by shock loading from the hard undercarriage inducing a fatigue failure of the rivets joining the spar booms to the wing structure.

1959 – a new design emerges

For many years the companies looked to their own salvation. By early 1959, just as Silver City Airways' searches for replacement equipment were into their final phase, their main competitor had been taking action of a more definite kind to ensure that the future of their business was assured when they too had to retire their aged Freighters from active service.

F.A. Laker, then Executive Director of British United Airways, had already realised that the amount of usage left on the Bristol Freighter for cross-Channel vehicle air ferry work was coming to an end, either because the Certificate of Airworthiness for the aircraft had been revalued as a result of the wing fatigue findings or that they were becoming less suited to the task as air traffic increased in volume or requirements. It was obvious that a successor had to be found if the services were not to die with the withdrawal from use of the type.

Foreseeing that the expanding services to be offered by the embryo company, Channel Air Bridge Limited, and other operators in the same line would require a new type of aircraft designed for just the air ferry task, and one that would not be made obsolete or rendered inoperative early in its life by design limitations or a change in the pattern of operations, Freddie Laker decided that clearly the answer was for the vehicle air ferry operators to seek their own solution to the problem. The solution was either to adapt a type already in use or, on a relatively low initial expenditure, produce a completely new design which had a fairly long life ahead of it to fill the role. The latter option proved impossible to achieve within the financial constraints placed on the project therefore it was decided to adapt an existing type at minimal cost.

Laker then contacted A.C. Leftley, Chief Design Engineer for Aviation Traders Engineering Limited, in January 1959 and asked for design studies to proceed on a replacement aircraft for the Bristol Freighter. The choice of Aviation Traders as the company to formulate the design, and indeed produce the aircraft, was logical in that in addition to being an associate member of the main British United Group group it had previously carried out conversion work on existing types for various users. Although a much smaller concern when compared with the larger and more major corporations it had nevertheless gained extensive and useful experience in the specialist field of airframe modifications, including the civilianisation of numerous Handley Page Halifax bombers to Halton standard for various airlines and private operators in the immediate post-Second World War period.

Another Aviation Traders (ATEL) project was the modifications carried out to Avro Tudors to convert them to the Super Trader pure freight aircraft by the addition of a large loading door in the port fuselage side, whilst in 1959 they were engaged in the civilianisation of a major part of a batch of 253 ex-RAF Percival Prentice three-seat training aircraft for sale onto the civil market.

No mention of past events in the history of Aviation Traders would be complete without the inclusion of a previous own-design by the company, the ATL90 Accountant. This type, intended as a replacement for the stalwart Douglas DC3, was conceived and built by ATEL at a time when the design team was comparatively young in experience on the more recent trends in component and airframe design. Although only the prototype Accountant flew it showed without doubt that the company was capable of designing and producing aircraft and components to a very high standard, and indeed the exhibiting of the type at the 1957 SBAC Farnborough Air Show showed the confidence the company had in its products.

The Bristol 170 Freighter Mk 32 'Superfreighter', predecessor to the Carvair, in this case G-AOUV seen at Calais-Marck in June 1959. Although it was a rugged and capable design its failings were the limited wing spar life arising as a direct result of shock loading from the hard undercarriage, the incapability to carry more than four vehicles at a time, and its inability to cope with long-distance services unless an intermediate refuelling stop was made en route. Whilst 'Channel Air Bridge' is shown inside the nose doors the aircraft was owned by Air Charter Ltd from December 1956 and on loan to Sabena at the time the picture was taken. Built in August 1956 by Bristol Aircraft with constructors number 13258 it carries the name 'Valour' and served on cross-Channel services from 1958 until scrapped in 1967.

Although Arthur Leftley was given free range to investigate every possible avenue Laker had already thought over in his rare leisure moments just what was available on the market to use, and intimated that in the end a return would be made to the Douglas C54 design and the modifications necessary to bring that aircraft to the new configuration.

The new requirements ideally suited the selection of a piston-engined aircraft as the idea of using turboprop or pure jet for this work was not at this stage in time considered in any detail. The type would be unpressurised as operating heights and service conditions would not warrant a pressure hull. All existing types were considered and studies made, these had to be capable of being modified easily without any chance of overstressing the basic design and be available in sufficient quantity and at reasonable cost. Engine and airframe spares also had to be easily obtainable, especially if the ultimate number of conversions was to prove worthwhile for full-scale production to commence.

Some existing types already in service were near enough the desired configuration but because they had been produced to fulfil different roles would have been found unsuitable in the final event for car ferry work for one reason or another. The Blackburn Beverley, or Universal Freighter, was considered quite early in the studies for its cavernous fuselage, which would easily have permitted a two-tier arrangement for passengers and vehicles or mixed freight, but the aircraft itself was too large to be used economically on the cross-channel routes, especially where smaller airfields were involved.

The Handley Page Hermes also looked promising with its large fuselage but, although the resulting layout seemed suitable, the type was rejected as snags on this included engine unsuitability and an insufficient quantity of airframes and spares. At the other end of the scale the Vickers Viscount was ruled out due to its small fuselage diameter.

The Hastings, from the same stable as the Hermes, was looked at in detail as it promised to be available on the civil market in enough quantity, but as the desired fuselage layout could not be realised without extensive rework of the structure it too was dismissed.

In the case of the Armstrong Whitworth Argosy, the AW650, the existing layout was almost perfect with the twin tail booms offering unrestricted access to the rear-opening freight doors; however the drawbacks in this case were the much shorter fuselage with its associated lower cubic density and the fact that the original design utilised turboprop power and a pressurised system.

After design studies had been carried out on all the aircraft proposed, the anticipated return was made to the Douglas C54 and the rework necessary to bring this type into line with the new specification. No work was envisaged being carried out at this time on the two other likely Douglas types, the DC4 and DC6, although design studies were completed when the ATL98 (as the new aircraft was to be known) was fully proven, as both of these were still in regular airline service and likely to cost much more to obtain and convert, whereas the C54 could be obtained from surplus-to-requirement or military stocks. Although these would probably be in a somewhat delapidated condition it would not be a cause for concern as the whole airframe would be recertified after conversion was complete.

With the C54 schemes before them the design team found everything falling more or less into place, the airframe being rugged enough for adaptation and of the right dimensions internally in both length and cross-section. It was also beneficial to use the C54 design as the powerplants, the Pratt & Whitney R2000 Twin Wasp, were easy to maintain and availability of spares in general was extremely good.

From the earlier design studies it had been concluded that a nose access for vehicles and freight into a full-length cargo hold would be utilised, with the passengers in a separate compartment to the rear of the aircraft. As to placing the cockpit area in a hinging nose it was decided that this would present as many problems with control system continuity and connection as would a hinging tail arrangement, so a layout was produced that was similar to the Argosy by which the cockpit area was elevated above the level of the main cargo hold. Crew access was to be from inside the fuselage and a separate nose loading door, not connected with the cockpit area, was to be employed.

The resulting shape of the front fuselage in the final design study for the C54 scheme was a rather bulbous affair with a long fairing to the rear of the flight deck (now situated quite high up in the air) and a large one-piece, sideways hinging door to the extreme front of the aircraft. The basic fuselage and wing components were to be virtually unchanged with the only heavy conversion work being on the front of the fuselage ahead of the wings.

Having now arrived at the desired layout for the new type, and before any further detailed design work could be carried out, Aviation Traders had to obtain written permission from the Douglas Aircraft

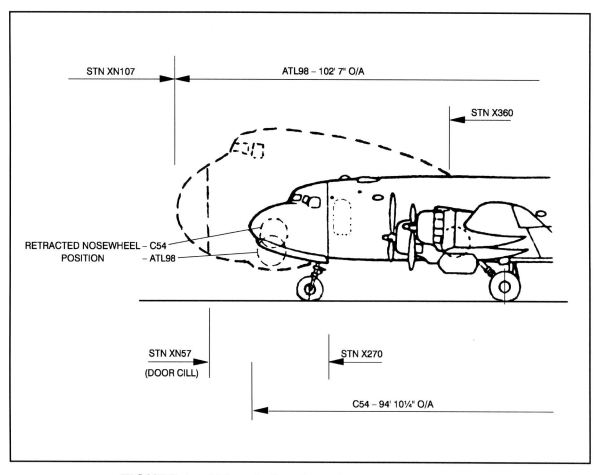

FIGURE 1 – ATL98 & C54 front fuselage comparison

Corporation, manufacturers of the C54 and DC4, for the use of their design. As it was not known how Douglas would react when approached with the request Arthur Leftley, in his capacity as Chief Designer, wrote directly to them to outline the project and asked for their views on the matter. He also advised that his arrival at their head office of Santa Monica on Western Island to discuss the matter in more detail would be shortly after their receipt of his letter. This approach was, in view of the time frame allowed for the design part of the project, intended to give Douglas no time to refuse the request for an interview.

On arrival at Santa Monica at the end of March 1959 Leftley was met by a very impressive array of company officials who each interviewed him in turn, all their questions being fairly comprehensive but intended to determine exactly how far Aviation Traders wanted to use and modify the C54 design. After numerous consultations lasting many hours it was agreed exactly how much information Aviation Traders required, and also to what extent the basic design would (and could) be modified, the Douglas executives then insisted that Leftley sign an agreement stating that the information loaned would be used for this one project only. This was to safeguard company interests, first so that another concern could only set up a limited production line involving a Douglas product, and secondly to absolve the Douglas company of any unseen problems and liabilities that might arise.

The cost of supplying the data and drawings was a further matter to be settled, for when this was discussed both parties had different ideas in mind. After Leftley had suggested the cost of reproduction could not be less than ten thousand, but certainly not more than one hundred thousand or the project would not go ahead, the Douglas directors conferred and agreed at a final price of ten thousand. However, whilst Leftley was thinking in terms of the pound Sterling, and Douglas the U.S. dollar, Aviation Traders had unknowingly reduced their initial expenditure by this misconstruing of the currency they were dealing in. At that moment in time, with the rate of exchange at 2.801 dollars to the pound, the cost for all the data came to less than £3,570. This solo excursion by ATEL changed their policy such that all later business trips of this type included for two persons, one to answer questions and the other to consider possible implications and other suggestions.

On his return to England in early April Leftley brought with him as much in the way of information that Douglas could amass at such short notice, which in the meantime would be enough to allow ATEL to continue with detailed design work. Under the terms of the joint agreement Douglas would send the rest of the data on the C54 once it was retrieved from their archives, production of the type having long since been discontinued, but while ATEL had based their design studies on the C54 it was in fact information on the DC4 that would form a major part of the material yet to come.

A long wait followed before ATEL received details of the DC4 loft lines as these were not now available, therefore as a temporary measure Santa Monica could only offer dimensional co-ordinates from which ATEL were able to plot the fuselage shape. These details were of course necessary in order to complete the drawings for the wind tunnel model which had to be made as soon as possible after Leftley returned from America in order to meet the deadline for use of the wind tunnel at the College of Aeronautics, Cranfield. It had been agreed that Aviation Traders, lacking such testing facilities of their own, could only use the Cranfield wind tunnel during the 1959 summer vacation and if the appointment was not met a further year would pass before a similar opportunity arose.

Straightway after Leftley's return from America manufacture of the wind tunnel model was put under way at Westway Models of London NW10, but it was not until June that the required loft lines finally arrived from Douglas. In July a last-minute rush then ensued to complete the model and the additional various test attachment sections, this finally finishing in time to meet the schedule for use of the wind tunnel. The rest of the design meanwhile was continuing apace, and was eventually to last from the summer of 1959 through to the autumn of 1960 when a full shop drawing issue was made.

In all, the wind tunnel was used for 74 runs in August and September, totalling 76 hours 33 minutes, as a result of which ATEL were able to arrive at a decision as to the shape and length of the front fuselage and its rear fairing, and also the size of fin and rudder required. Before starting wind tunnel tests it was thought that the humped upper fuselage would create an unknown amount of buffet in flight that would exhaust the airflow before it reached the tail, but after trials with different fairing shapes on the model the ideal shape was achieved. Unexpectedly the fairing line to the upper deck provided a bonus not anticipated for its shape, being curved much like an aerofoil, induced a certain amount of body lift which, associated with a noticeable nose up change in pitch, brought about a 2½% forward shift of the neutral centre of gravity position. Thus an increase in speed over the original design was possible in the transition to a normal level flight position, and in order to achieve the same standard of longitudinal stability as the Douglas DC4 the centre of gravity for the ATL98 was finally established 4% forward in relation to that of the DC4.

ATEL were prepared initially to add endplates to the horizontal tail surfaces in order to provide additional fin area, as slipstream effect was an unknown factor and it was thought that any vortices created around the front fuselage would tend to grow in intensity during yaw with excessive rudder deflection and be directed onto the endplates. The idea of using endplates was dropped as these would have involved further work in stiffening a redesigned tailplane layout, the only changes made being to the fin which was squared off and capped, and with its overall height increased by 2' 10" a shape similar to that of the Douglas DC7C was arrived at. This produced a further bonus in that the rudder was made more effective; subsequently on flight trials with the prototype after conversion, rudder travel was reduced to sixteen degrees, a decrease of 20% from the original twenty degrees of the DC4.

In order to illustrate the complexity of tests carried out on the ATL98 wind tunnel model a summary of the runs made at Cranfield is shown in Table 1. As ATEL records for this were unobtainable at the time of writing these details were compiled from his personal files by Brian Kerry, Chief Aerodynamicist for Aviation Traders Engineering Ltd.

TABLE 1 – Summary of wind tunnel tests carried out at the College of Aeronautics, Cranfield in August and September 1959

Run No.	Nose	Fairing	Fin	Extra Dorsal	Tailplane	Endplates	Test
1	DC-4	Nil	DC-4	Nil	DC-4	Nil	Airspeed calibration
2							Forces with incidence
3							Moments with incidence
4							Forces with incidence
5							Moments with incidence
6							Flow visualisation
7							ditto
8							ditto
9							ditto
10							ditto
11							ditto
12							Forces with incidence
13							Moments with incidence
14							Forces with incidence
15							ditto
16							ditto (plus flow study)
17							Forces and moments with yaw
18	ATL98	J2 Mod 1					Forces with incidence
19							Flow study
20							ditto
21							ditto (plus photographs)
22							Forces with incidence
23							Moments with incidence
24							(Run omitted)
25							Flow study
26							ditto
27							ditto
28							ditto
29							Forces and moments with yaw
30							Flow study
31		J1					ditto
32							ditto
33		Nil	Extension 1				Moments with yaw
34	DC-4						ditto
35	ATL98	J2 Mod 1	DC-4	1			ditto
36			Nil				ditto
37			DC-4	Nil			ditto
38							Forces and moments with yaw
39					Extended	Medium	Moments with yaw
40							Forces and moments with incidence

6

Table 1 (continued)

Run No.	Nose	Fairing	Fin	Extra Dorsal	Tailplane	Endplates	Test
41	ATL98	J2 Mod 1	DC-4	Nil	DC-4	Nil	Lift curve slope of tailplane
42			Extension 1	2			Moments with yaw
43				2a			ditto
44				3			ditto
45							ditto
46							ditto
47							Forces and moments with incidence
48							ditto
49				4			Forces with yaw
50			DC-4				Moments with yaw
51			Nil				Forces with yaw
52			DC-4				ditto
53				Nil	Nil		Moments with incidence
54							Forces with incidence
55	DC-4	Nil			DC-4		Pressure distribution on fairing
56			Nil				dcm/dcl at 24° yaw
57			Nil	Nil			Forces with yaw
58	ATL98	J2 Mod 1					Moments with yaw
59			Extension 1	3			Forces with incidence
60							Moments with incidence
61		J2 Mod 2					Pitot rake on fairing and fuselage
62							Pressure distribution on fairing
63							Pitot rake on fairing
64		J2 Mod 3					Forces and moments with incidence
65							Forces with incidence
66		J2 Mod 2a					Total head plot
67							Forces and moments with incidence
68							Pressure plot on fairing
69		J2 Mod 3					Forces with incidence
70							Moments with incidence
71		J2 Mod 1	DC-4	Nil			Forces and moments with incidence
72			DC-4				Forces with incidence
73			Nil				ditto
74	DC-4		DC-4				ditto
75							ditto

Total run time in wind tunnel – 76 hours 33 minutes

The upper picture shows the ATL98 model with the normal length fuselage 'hump' and a dorsal extension to the extended fin, as used on test runs 44 to 49 in the Cranfield wind tunnel. This model later went on display at the Historic Aircraft Museum, Southend.

The lower shows the same fin profile but an extended upper deck, as used on runs 62 to 66.

(ATEL photos via A.C. Leftley)

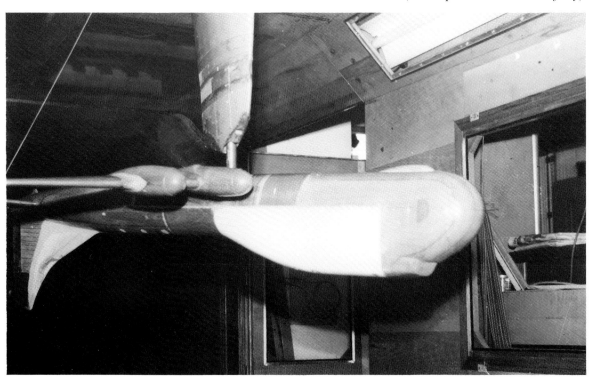

As only one wind tunnel model was available and used throughout the tests it was essential to fix the various shaped fuselage sections and control surfaces quickly but securely for each test run. Dowel locating pins were used, and any imperfections at the joint filled with plasticine in order to give true results. Whilst these on-site modifications prompted some thoughts as to possible further shape testing for the prototype they were in fact only used to produce a cleaner airflow shape for the tunnel.

It was also necessary to use plasticine infill to extend the rear edges of the fuselage fairing shape to finish further down the fuselage sides at a point where the cross-section returned to that of the original DC4. When attaching the various loose shapes to the basic fuselage during tunnel work it was found that the projected lines of the final test section would, on intersection with the original fuselage section between the top quarters and the horizontal axis, bring about a complex curved area of skinning and make production of the fuselage skin panels here impossible. As it was, the shapes eventually arrived at were found to be complicated enough for the production shop to keep up with.

When the results of the wind tunnel tests were analysed it was decided that no further research into the projected new shape would be necessary, accordingly the configuration as lofted and manufactured was as follows:–

Nose – ATL98	Top fairing – J2 Mod 2
Fin extension – 1	Additional dorsal – none
Tailplane – DC4	Endplates on tailplane – none.

It will be noticed from the run sequence chart that this configuration was not in fact flown in the wind tunnel, but Aviation Traders had gained enough knowledge of the various other shapes to be able to use this one with confidence. This was of course based on the premise that the pre-modification test flights, due to take place shortly on the first C54 acquired for the ATL98 programme, would arrive at a satisfactory conclusion and that the post-modification flights on the first conversion produce no unfavourable flight characteristics. In any event the production shop drawings were at this time in an advanced state and any further revisions would not have retarded progress significantly towards the final issue.

When the runs for the desired shape were complete ATEL then carried out further tests during this same period of tunnel use which included for an extended upper deck and the possible conversion of the DC6, but this was as far as these exercises went.

1960 – Pre-conversion test flights on the C54

Prior to acquiring the first C54 for pre-conversion work the detailed design programme had progressed rapidly with most snags being ironed out without undue time delays, but one obstacle still remained in the matter of the absence of recent flight test data for the C54 which Aviation Traders had to have for the purpose of comparing performance of the aircraft after it was modified to the new configuration. Requests for this information were made repeatedly to Douglas Aircraft Corporation, but as no recent tests had been carried out on the C54 they had to resort to their files in order to amass the necessary material.

Data was eventually received from Douglas at Santa Monica, but this was accurate only in that it related to a prime condition C54. It was known that G-ANYB, the first aircraft to arrive, was by now a very old airframe with over 37,000 flying hours and fifteen years service behind it and its present performance could not be considered as being similar to the original brochure figures. As the Douglas data could only be referred to, and not used during evaluation of each newly-converted aircraft, it was decided to carry out a short but intense programme of flight tests with 'NYB before any modification work was commenced, the results of which would then form the basis for a comparison of test results on other aircraft subsequently produced.

In mid-September 1960, after a long ferry flight from New York via Shannon, the first Douglas C54 arrived in England for its last days before conversion to ATL98 standard. In command was Captain Mackenzie, chief pilot for Aviation Traders, with Mike Jennings as First Officer, and Freddie Laker on board to ensure that the new acquisition arrived safely. The aircraft, a C54B with constructors number 10528, was delivered to Stansted and into the charge of Aviation Traders, although still in the ownership of Air Charter Ltd, with whom it had been operated as G-ANYB on major European and Atlantic air routes from January 1955 up to the time it was ceded to the ATL98 programme. When evaluation of it, as the first ATL98 to be built, was complete it was to be handed over to Channel Air Bridge to form the nucleus of the new vehicle air ferry fleet.

At this stage in time Aviation Traders had no facilities by way of company test pilots, but this was rectified soon after the arrival of G-ANYB by the employment of D.B. Cartlidge, a graduate of the Empire Test Pilots School at Farnborough. Having decided at this time to terminate his appointment as personal pilot for Lord Derby, when based at Liverpool, the advertisement placed in the aviation press seemed an opportune way of staying in the flying world and getting a change of scenery. Don Cartlidge applied for the post and was engaged as test pilot for the evaluation period of the new type, as well as being responsible for all flight crew training for the airlines when they took delivery of their aircraft.

On 21 September 1960, the day before Cartlidge joined the Aviation Traders team, the first pre-conversion flight was carried out on G-ANYB. In the absence of the programme test pilot Captain Robert Langley DFC, chief pilot and managing captain for Channel Air Bridge, made this check although he was not cleared to proceed with a full set of flight trials until later in the proceedings. P. Drescher, Ken Smith and A.M. Wallis made up the rest of the crew on this flight, which lasted just one hour and was to check the aircraft's performance in the critical engine-out configuration with flaps at 15° and the undercarriage in both the extended and retracted configurations.

The remaining flights, varying from two to five hours duration and for a specific objective, were captained mainly by Don Cartlidge, and are detailed below:

Flight 2 (22 September) – stalls in various configurations of flaps and undercarriage, in turns and at various power settings (3 hrs 5 mins).
(crew – R. Langley, D. Cartlidge, K. Smith, P. Drescher)

Flight 3 (24 September) – sideslips in various configurations, yaw with assymetric power, baulked landings (4 hrs 40 mins).
(crew – R. Langley, D. Cartlidge, K. Smith, R. Salvage)

Flight 4 (29 September) – performance climbs in various flight configurations from varying starting heights (4 hrs 50 mins)
(crew – R. Langley, A.M. Wallis, K. Smith, P. Drescher)

Flight 5 (29 September) – handling under ARB captaincy. Stalls, stability, sideslips, change of stick force with flap and power, longitudinal stability, baulked landing (2 hrs 5 mins)
(crew – G. Howitt & R. Bryder (A.R.B), D. Cartlidge, R. Langley, K. Smith)

Flight 6 (3 October) – stalls, trim speeds, baulked landings (2 hrs)
(crew – D. Cartlidge, R. Langley, K. Smith, B. Kerry)

The pre-conversion test flights, interspersed with discussions and calculations relating to the tests, were spread over a period of thirteen days and amassed a total flying time of 17 hrs 40 mins. This was made up of 10 hrs 30 mins spent on performance checks and 7 hrs 10 mins on aircraft handling capability. At this stage of the programme both Don Cartlidge and Bob Langley, and flight test engineer Ken Smith, were completely satisfied with the results and able to report to the design team that G-ANYB had performed more or less in accordance with the manufacturer's tabled figures (allowing for the age of the aeroplane) and, having established a standard to work to for the post-conversion tests, gave clearance for work to proceed in dismantling the airframe for conversion.

Producing the prototype

After its last flight as a C54 on 3 October 'NYB landed back at the municipal airport of Southend where Aviation Traders put it into their 'black shed', the hangar where all the conversion work for this, the prototype ATL98, was to be centred. The finished product was to be virtually a new aircraft so every item had to be removed for inspection, and if found to be unserviceable or not required the situation was to be amended as necessary. This reasoning applied particularly to items which had to be fitted or changed in order to comply with Board of Trade requirements.

The engines, Pratt & Whitney R2000 Twin Wasps, were removed and all four sent away complete to the Bristol Siddeley Engine Company for each to be individually run on the test rigs there, however by contrast with the previous flight trials the results from these engine tests were of a very different nature. Whilst running each engine it was found that the power achieved at maximum cylinder head temperature (CHT) was not as stated in the manufacturer's brochure, being down by exactly 100 bhp to 1350 bhp. The brochure figure of 1450 bhp **could** be achieved only by exceeding the maximum CHT, but as this condition would never be experienced in service use the lower figure was adopted. As it was, Aviation Traders were only concerned with the figures applicable to the maximum take-off power condition where the CHT would govern. This was the first time the Twin Wasp had been evaluated by anyone other than Pratt & Whitney and found to be under-performing but the matter was not pursued and put down to the age of the engines, the figure of 1350 bhp being used as the basis for comparative checks on engines fitted after conversion and to later aircraft modified to ATL98 standard.

It is worth noting that during the exhaustive testing of the engines only one actually failed whilst on the test rigs, this being replaced by another calibrated unit in order to make up the quota of four required to be refitted to G-ANYB for the flight trials after conversion.

The replacement engine was installed in the number four position with the existing number four moved to the position of the failed number three unit.

Prior to dismantling G-ANYB for conversion the fuel system lines and tanks were drained, plus the necessary removal of electrical power and depressurisation of the various hydraulic systems. Both mainplanes were removed outboard of the engines so that the wing-mounted fuel tanks and associated system fittings could be removed, these were then overhauled and refitted to the new requirements. These operations also allowed x-ray tests to be made on the wing spars and fuel tanks, the wing spars needing many stainless steel doubler plates to reinforce defective sections where skin corrosion was found.

Also removed complete were the tail control surfaces, fin and horizontal stabilizer, the fin and rudder being dealt with especially to embody the modifications necessary to build them up to the new shape. The rudder remained the same height but was reworked to square off the top whereas the fin was increased in height by 2' 10" and the top given a flattened but slightly curving line. The leading edge of the fin was also reworked to a straight line with the addition of a section between the existing fin station 135 and a new station 193.

At an early stage it was decided that retention of the original floor, being of a continuous corrugated metal construction, would be a disadvantage to vehicle ferry operations due to the need to be able to remove sections of it for cleaning underneath. These floor sections would have to be of a size capable of handling by one man and it was also realised that they would have to be fitted with a facility for differing locations of tie-down for various sizes of vehicles. This facility would have to be capable of being fixed quickly in service but readily adaptable to allow for angled tie-down and of adequate strength to cater for most vehicle axle loads.

After testing various materials and investigating the methods of fixing these down to the underfloor structure it was decided to use a composite deck employing a plywood top face, aluminium alloy bottom face and an infill of Plasticell to produce a panel ¾" thick. Ranging in size between 5' 0" and 8' 0" in length and approximately 3' 3" wide the panels, all having unreinforced edges, were fixed down with 10/32" diameter bolts onto an inverted top hat section framework which was in turn carried on the fuselage floor cross beams. Into each floor panel were fixed the vehicle tie-down or freight lashing anchorage points, these being a loose D-ring held down by a retaining block into a recessed mounting plate with a large circular plate washer on the underside located in a recessed mounting plate similar to that on top. The entire freight hold and part of the rear passenger cabin had 96 such points.

The lashing straps were made of high-strength webbing with quick-release snaphooks at the ends, and for the tie-down of vehicles were simply strapped around the wheel and axle end. In service use these straps were to prove so effective at restraining fore and aft wheel movements that no other device or wheel chock was found necessary.

Having decided to use a completely new floor, the existing floor was removed and disposed of as scrap. In the case of G-ANYB the freight floor, having been subjected to so much adverse treatment, was in such condition that reuse of any part of it would not have been worthwhile, accordingly the new floor system was fitted throughout the entire fuselage area from the new front loading door cill to the bulkhead relocated at the rear of the passenger compartment at fuselage station X905 to give a total hold length of 80' 2".

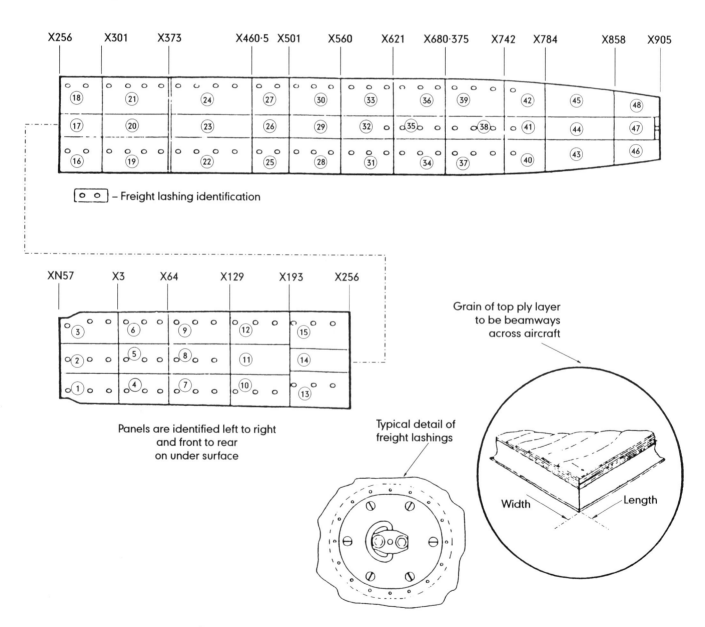

FIGURE 2 – Floor panel and freight lashing layout

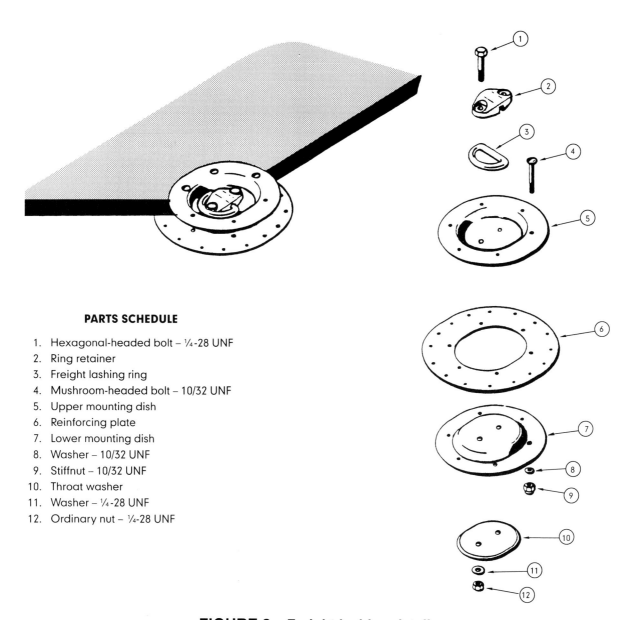

PARTS SCHEDULE

1. Hexagonal-headed bolt – ¼-28 UNF
2. Ring retainer
3. Freight lashing ring
4. Mushroom-headed bolt – 10/32 UNF
5. Upper mounting dish
6. Reinforcing plate
7. Lower mounting dish
8. Washer – 10/32 UNF
9. Stiffnut – 10/32 UNF
10. Throat washer
11. Washer – ¼-28 UNF
12. Ordinary nut – ¼-28 UNF

FIGURE 3 – Freight lashing details

When other items of pre-conversion dismantling were complete work began on removal of the unwanted C54 nose from the rest of the structure. The fuselage was levelled up off the floor on trestles and, all controls and systems passing rearwards from the cockpit area now having been disconnected, the control columns and pedals, centre pedestals and seats were removed for overhaul and subsequent reinstallation after conversion.

Removal of the original nose structure was effected by removing the fuselage skinning and cutting through the stringers. The cut line in the vertical plane was forward of fuselage station X270 and ran from stringers 33 on the centre underside upwards to include mid-height stringers 18 on both sides. From this level the cut was taken horizontally rearwards through the fuselage frames back to station X360, then finally extended vertically up to the fuselage topside. Fuselage stringers in the jointing area were cut to exact length projections and cleaned up in preparation for mating with those to be left projecting from the rear of the new front fuselage. The Douglas station numbers on the original fuselage were retained and prefixed 'X', whilst those on the new front fuselage and forward of station '0' were prefixed 'XN'. Thus the fuselage was renumbered from XN107 at the extreme front of the nose loading door, back through XN57 at the fuselage door cill and X0 under the cockpit to X1123·5 at the extreme rear.

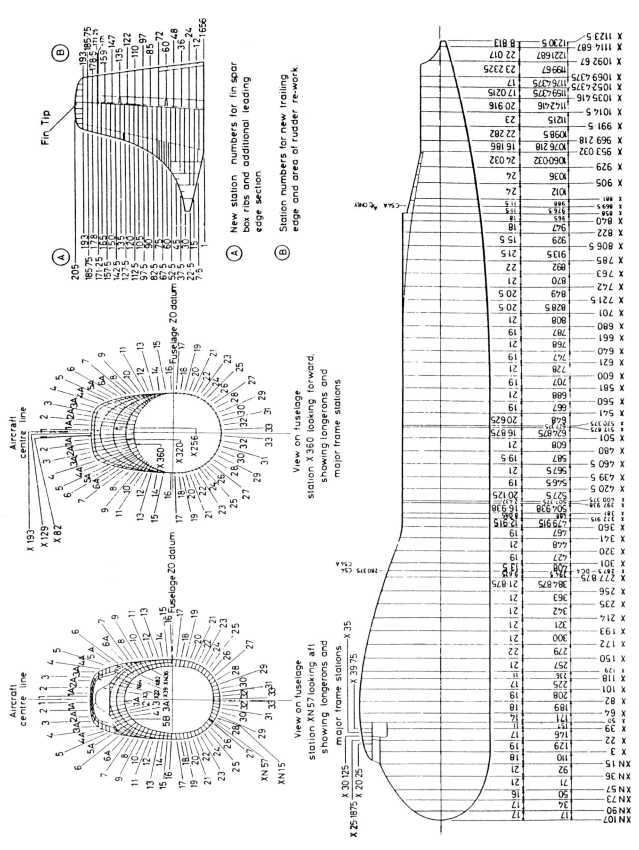

FIGURE 4 – Fuselage station numbers for ATL98

Front fuselage unit

The new front fuselage unit itself was built in three sections split horizontally. The upper section contained the cockpit floor and glazing frames along with the rear framing plus half frames XN57 to X360 and stringers 1 to 9 with the lower section having the freight deck level support beams plus half frames XN57 to X256 and stringers 17 to 33. To fill in the gap between the upper and lower sections side panels of 0.028" (0.7 mm) thick plate were fixed over the lapped and jointed fuselage frame ends left projecting from both the top and bottom of the two front fuselage halves from stations XN57 back to station X360. These sections, applied on both sides, were the last to be fixed to complete the structural unit.

Each of the two main halves was initially built up with stringers and half frames on a construction jig and the skinning, each piece hand-shaped, fixed to it. Construction and buildup of the new front fuselage sections did not present so much of a problem as the skinning-up of the unit. The new shape presented the metal skinners with very complex changes of angles through which the top panels between fuselage stations X129 and X360 had to be worked, and to a lesser degree the panels around the nose door stations.

The complex panel shapes were formed by the skinners on a wheeling horse, a simple item but one which could not have been replaced by production tools as it was not known if the final number of conversions in the sales order book would warrant the expenditure. It later transpired that this method was adopted for the manufacture of all further front fuselage units when full production commenced in 1961.

Connection of the two fuselage halves at frame X360 was critical in that this frame was the springing-off point for the fairing to the rear of the elevated crew compartment. New half frames fitted to the rear of the front fuselage unit between stations X277·875 and X360 supported the complicated skinned sections, the rearmost frame locating with the frame at station X360 on the rear fuselage. When connecting the upper and lower halves of the front fuselage unit together using the side panel sections the halves were jigged up in position one above the other, and the side plates and splicing members fitted to frame up the basic structure.

As soon as the structure was finished the installation fitters moved in to fix the cockpit instruments, fixtures and fittings. Most of the fittings reinstalled were those taken from the original C54 nose section and included seats, controls and control columns, thus the revised cockpit layout was not much different to that of the C54 except the flight crew would be able to enjoy a more roomy 'office'.

Entry to the elevated flight deck was by means of a vertical ladder from the freight deck, this being fixed on the starboard fuselage sidewall and leading up to a hatch in the flight deck floor. Hinged to swing upwards the hatch was kept open by spring clips fitted to the sidewall, and in the closed position a simple ball catch held the hatch down and flush with the flight deck floor. Normally this hatch was the crew exit from the flight deck, but for emergency use an escape hatch 21½" x 31½" was installed in the flight deck ceiling. The escape hatch, fitted with a green-tinted perspex centre panel, was located on the aircraft centreline and could be opened from inside or outside the aircraft.

Windscreens

Cockpit glazing installed in the new front fuselage was that as previously fitted to the now-discarded C54 nose section but refitted in a new configuration and framework. Due to a slightly wider cockpit and rearranged instrumentation it was not possible to utilise the old frame so a new frame was produced in order to reuse the original glazing. Front screens, after cleaning up, were installed with the central pillar at fuselage station XN15 (two new frames aft of the nose door opening) and sloped outwards to join stringer No 4 at station X20, the opening side windows then being fitted flush with the fuselage side lines between stations X20 and X39.

The upper section of a front fuselage unit being built up in the jigs at Southend. The flight deck floor formed the bottom level of this section. Note the wooden mallet and tea cup at left front – two essential items of equipment! *(ATEL photo via A.C. Leftley)*

Nose loading door

The new nose loading door occupied the extreme front of the fuselage between stations XN57 and XN107 and comprised a single-piece, hydraulically-operated unit hinging on the port side at station XN57 to pivot through 180° for loading cargo. Construction employed a spheroidal ribbed frame with strengthening cross members onto which were riveted the shaped alloy outer skin panels. On the inside lower edge of the door a shelf was installed level with the freight deck, this was generally used for the stowage of surplus fitments and freight lashings. From the shelf edge down to the door bottom a vertical panel was fitted to butt against that on the fuselage when the door was closed.

In the centre at the extreme front of the door was the main air intake for the heating and ventilation system, internally this was ducted diagonally up to the top port side and mated with a similar duct on the fuselage at station XN57 when the door was closed. Set behind transparent windows in the lower part of the forward face of the door were two taxi-ing lights, these were fixed and supplemented the normal landing lights installed in the wings.

Because of the size and position of the door above ground level it was decided that manual operation could not be easily carried out, therefore a handpump was fitted just inside the fuselage adjacent to the door cill on the starboard side and connected hydraulically to an operating jack at the top of the door. After selecting the required operating direction the handpump was vigorously worked back and forth to either open or close the door. Two fluid cylinders were fitted to the handpump which was of Lockheed manufacture and, at the expense of increasing the number of strokes and length of time to move the door, pumping pressure could be reduced to aid the operator by the removal of a pip-pin which freed one cylinder and left only one operative. This feature was useful in strong winds up to 45 mph (52 kts), this being the limiting factor for operating the door without any overstressing of the hydraulic system. With the door closed twin locating pins on the door engaged catches on the fuselage, microswitches fitted at the door edges indicating the latch mechanism was fully engaged by illuminating warning lights in the cockpit.

The front fuselage of G-ANYB being finished in the jig at Southend, work being centred on the nose loading door. Note the extensive use of 'Dexion' angle as supports for the structure.

(ATEL photo via Terry Leighton)

Nose landing gear

To house the nose landing gear presented Aviation Traders with another minor problem for as the freight floor now ran fully aft from the new nose door cill it was obvious that the previous arrangement by Douglas of allowing the nosewheel to retract 19 degrees above the horizontal into the fuselage could not be employed again. The basic nose landing gear unit was unchanged, indeed the whole undercarriage 'footprint' was the same, except for the use of DC6-type single-disc brakes in lieu of the multiple-disc of the C54 and a minor change in the nosewheel geometry by way of a reduction in travel of the actuating strut.

The geometry change was effected by the fitting of a 5·45" long steel tube as a stop on the piston rod of the actuating strut, which reduced the nosegear sweep from the original 94 degrees to 75. To also ensure that the strut cleared the underside of the floor structure when in operation the yoke end pivot at station X118 was moved down 4" lower than on the C54, and brought the retracted noseleg to a horizontal position at a vertical dimension of ZN64·5, below fuselage datum of Z0. As the lower portion of the retracted nosewheel was now outside the main fuselage line pod-shaped doors were fitted between stations X3 and X129 to fair over the wheel and damping piston.

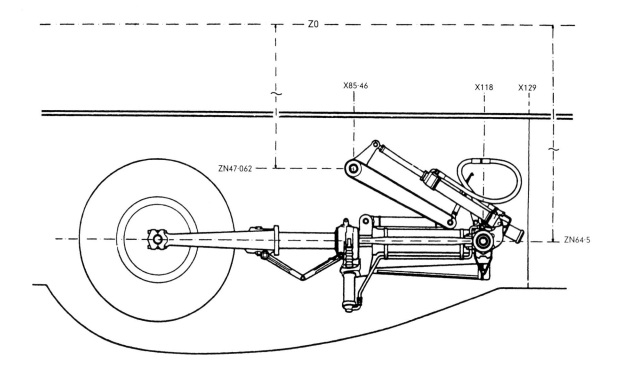

FIGURE 5 – Retracted nose landing gear

Control cable routing

Due to the elevated flight deck it was necessary to revise the arrangement for the main and accessory control cable routes in order to run each circuit down into the fuselage to the point where they could rejoin the original C54 layout. Cable continuity itself presented no problems but the revised routing had its share of snags until the patterns were able to link up with the existing C54 entry points to the wings and tail unit. The elevator cable circuit was the easiest to achieve for, with the original control columns reinstalled, the cables ran directly aft at high level in the fuselage until the tailplane location was reached. Here they cranked down over two sets of pulleys either side of the beam at station X953 then linked up to the elevator operating arm.

Cable routing to the wings was slightly more difficult to achieve. A total of 96 main and accessory cables ran from existing selectors aft to station X50 where they split into port and starboard runs each containing 48 cables in groups. At intervals between stations X129 and X193 each group then turned horizontally through 90 degrees and ran out to the cabin sidewalls. At this point another turn took the cables down to follow the fuselage sidewalls radially, using mid-height pulleys, until below freight floor level where they rose slightly and returned underfloor to the fuselage centreline. Here staggered 90-degree turns then brought each group horizontal once more to connect with the original C54 routing between stations X260 – X280. The aileron trim cable circuit followed a similar route but only on the starboard side.

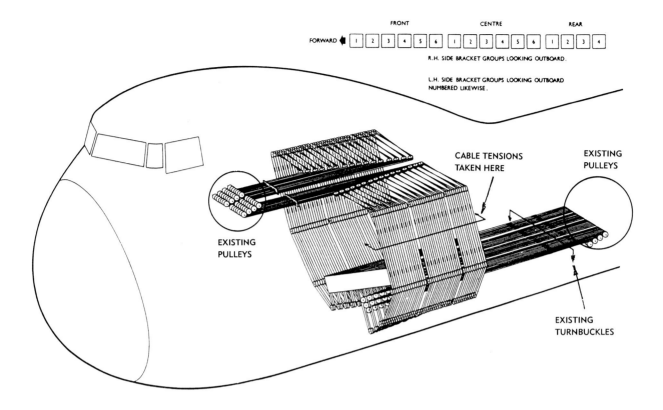

FRONT   CENTRE   REAR

FORWARD [1][2][3][4][5][6] [1][2][3][4][5][6] [1][2][3][4]

R.H. SIDE BRACKET GROUPS LOOKING OUTBOARD.

L.H. SIDE BRACKET GROUPS LOOKING OUTBOARD
NUMBERED LIKEWISE.

CABLE TENSIONS
TAKEN HERE

EXISTING
PULLEYS

EXISTING
PULLEYS

EXISTING
TURNBUCKLES

FIGURE 6 – Modified area of accessory controls

In order to achieve the six changes of direction for each control circuit, and transfer the entire run of 97 main and accessory cables down from the flight deck to the underfloor without infringing into the freight hold, many hundreds of cast brackets and approximately 600 extra control pulleys were installed between fuselage stations X50 (at cockpit level) and X280 (underfloor). When the front fuselage was first laid out on paper it was realised that a considerable underfloor space would be needed to accommodate the control pulleys and their support beams, and although everything was eventually contained within an 18" zone this increased the overall height of the fuselage and emphasised the fairing shape.

All the basic wing and mid-fuselage control circuits on the ATL98 remained the same as for the C54 and DC4 in that they were mechanically operated, and it said a lot for Aviation Traders when it was found that the average friction on each re-routed circuit was only in the order of 1½ lbs, and that no lost motion was apparent. Adjustments to cable tensions were effected between fuselage stations X235 and X265 for the wing-mounted systems and the elevator circuit, with the elevator trim circuit checked at station X540. All the original C54 circuit fittings or overhauled replacements were used in the same positions as before, including the various servos fitted to the autopilot and flight control circuits.

Instrumentation

The basic instrument system remained virtually unchanged except for the re-positioning of some indicators and the addition of others to the main instrument panel. Some instruments were sited on a redesigned starboard console panel and a left-hand header panel. A 28-volt DC electrical supply was installed for radio operation with 19 volts available from the main bus bar for some equipment, otherwise the system was identical to that of the C54.

A front fuselage unit at Southend with skinning complete. The lighter panels at mid-height are the infill skin plates between the upper and lower sections. From the rear of the frame at station X270 the stringers are left over-length, those on the upper half having yet to be extended a further 7'6" prior to mating with the parent C54 fuselage. *(ATEL photo via A.C. Leftley)*

Intercom

An Ultra intercom system (from the 19 volt supply) was installed with a jack plug point in the nose wheel bay for ground crew intercommunication with the crew on the flight deck.

Lighting

In the rear passenger cabin there were no individual lights but the concealed roof lights, three on each side of the cabin, gave excellent general lighting for reading. Passengers had dimming controls for these lights.

Cabin air conditioning and heating system

Individual cold air louvres were provided for each row of seats, and cabin heating came via a single 100,000 BthU Dragonair combustion heater, instead of the twin Janitrol system of the DC4 and C54, which also served the flight deck. Warm air was admitted to the seating areas through floor level grilles in the front and rear cabin bulkheads.

Rear compartment and service facilities

A staggered bulkhead to separate the rear cabin from the freight hold was installed across the front of the rear compartment. This followed a line from fuselage station X742 on the starboard side to approximately the aircraft centreline then extended forward to X721·5 to accommodate the enclosure for the passenger service items, including the galley.

The galley, situated at the rear end of the entrance passageway, was of compact layout and contained adequate facilities for passenger services on the proposed cross-Channel usage. Hot drinks were provided for by the installation of a 2-gallon (10 litre) GEC beverage container and stowage was possible for food boxes, bottles, glasses and the other necessary items in the not-too-generous amount of space available.

The bulkhead extended forward of the galley to where a sliding door between X721·5 and X661 gave access from the entrance passageway to the main cargo hold. In the car ferry configuration with up to 22 passengers in the rear cabin seating for the stewardess, or cabin attendant, was catered for by the provision of a tip-up seat in the passageway. This seat, situated forward of the passenger entry door on the sidewall just opposite the sliding door into the main cargo hold, was fitted with an adjustable seatbelt and intended primarily for use during takeoff and landing.

At the extreme forward end of the entrance passageway an inward-opening door led into the toilet compartment, this being of the same width as the corridor and extending from frame X661 forward to frame X600. Although again of small size it contained the required toilet and washing facilities along with towel dispensers and containers for disposals. The toilet unit itself was a recirculating chemical type and required no external water supply for flushing, merely opening and closing the lid operated a pump to dispense the disinfectant solution. Easy removal of the unit from the aircraft for contents disposal was allowed for.

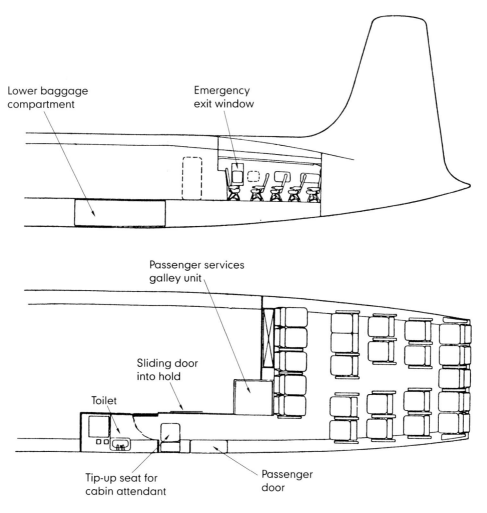

FIGURE 7 – Passenger compartment, 23-seat layout

A hot and cold water supply was installed to the washbasin, with a GEC ½-kilowatt water heater fitted to the hot water circuit and situated under the washbasin. Electrical power for the heater was drawn from the rear distribution bus, with a warning light connected across the heater elements to indicate when it was in operation.

Passenger seating

Seat fixings were installed at freight deck level in the rear passenger compartment and the floor tracks for these were flush with the removable floor panels to give an uninterrupted smooth floor line. Each seat unit was secured in position by floor attachments incorporated in the seat legs which engaged in constant-pitch holes in the floor tracks. The lengths of track not being used for seating at any time were merely covered over with the carpet laid throughout the passenger area.

The seats, designed to the specification laid down by Aviation Traders, were manufactured by Flying Services Engineering and Equipment Ltd, of Chesham, Buckinghamshire. Each unit consisted of a non-reclining, welded tubular steel construction with break-back, tip-up seat and pan and had one armrest fitted (the armrest for the wallside seat was fixed to the cabin sidewall). Seat width was 15½" and the complete assemblies, installed at 30" pitch, were designed to be stressed to 9G loading. Weights of seat units were modest, with the rearward-facing four-seat unit being 95·8 lbs, and the forward-facing two, three and five-seat units being 39·25, 57·75 and 90 lbs respectively. When the all-passenger versions of the ATL98 were used by British Air Ferries and other operators from 1969 onwards all the seating forward of bulkhead X758 was of a different type, every seat being fitted with two armrests each having a concealed ashtray.

Emergency equipment

Emergency equipment fitted in the flight deck area comprised a portable fire extinguisher and an axe installed on the starboard sidewall plus two escape ropes, one located near the emergency exit on the left-hand side just aft of the windscreen and the other next to the overhead escape hatch, and an emergency light at the highest point on the flight deck ceiling. Pouches for the stowage of emergency torches and a Very pistol, with its spare cartridges, were also provided on the flight deck.

The rear passenger cabin was catered for by the installation of an escape rope and exit chute at the main entrance door, another escape rope next to the starboard escape hatch and a portable fire extinguisher just inside the main entrance door. Emergency torches and a first aid kit were stowed in pouches near the escape hatch rope.

Further portable fire extinguishers and an axe were also installed in the main freight hold, all the portable extinguishers used throughout the aircraft being of the Graviner type 25H pattern and charged with methyl bromide.

To control in-flight engine fires the mechanically-operated carbon dioxide protection system of the C54 was retained. The system as reinstalled used existing components and controls fitted in similar positions to the C54 layout but with one mandatory modification. For all ATL98s operating under British registry it was required that methyl bromide extinguishers should protect Zone 1 of each engine, and be operated by electrical inertia switches in the event of the aircraft force-landing. The cabin heater fire extinguisher, again of the methyl bromide type, was installed adjacent to the nose door cill on the port side.

Fire warnings would be given on visual and audible indicators from fire detectors installed in the engine bays, forward accessories compartment and the underfloor baggage hold.

For illumination of the aircraft interior in the event of a main electrical circuit failure five inertia-operated emergency lights were fitted, two on the rear cabin ceiling, one by each exit and one in the flight deck ceiling.

FRONT FUSELAGE EQUIPMENT

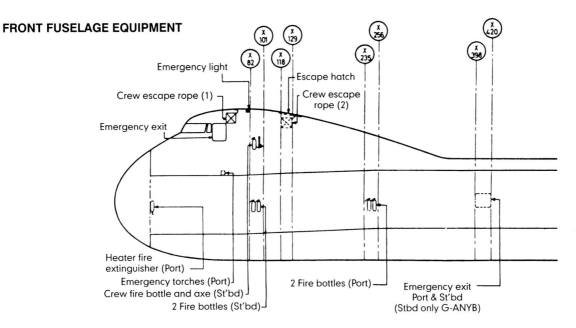

REAR FUSELAGE EQUIPMENT

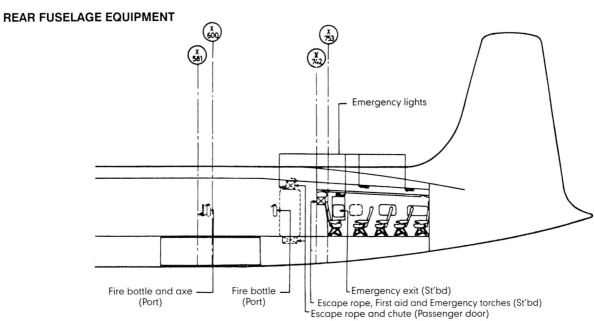

REAR CABIN EQUIPMENT AND EXITS

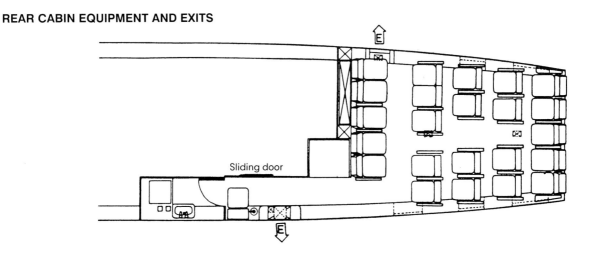

FIGURE 8 – Emergency equipment and exits

The Hylo Loaders

Developed in parallel with the ATL98 were the loaders necessary to transfer vehicles and freight between ground level and the aircraft door cill, a height between 9' 4" and 10' 0" in the loaded and empty conditions respectively. This height factor precluded the use of ramps such as were employed for the Bristol Freighter, and although early thoughts and sketches showed models of the ATL98 with similar types these would have been extremely long and impractical to use in service. A separate section of ATEL, which later became their heavy engineering division, took over the old BKS hangar at Southend (after the demise of that company) as the design and production centre for the vehicle and freight loaders soon to become a common sight around the car-ferry bases. These were a self-contained lifting unit initially used just for vehicle ferry work but in later service they were to load all manner of freight, the details below being released when the first Hylo, as the Mk 1 unit was called, made its appearance.

The Hylo was initially supplied in two basic versions, one a self-propelled unit powered by a 558 cc J.A.P. petrol engine and weighing 3·8 tons, the other a towed version with no built-in power facilities weighing 3·3 tons. Both had a safe working load of 5 tons, and although the Hylo was available in the two basic forms its platform and wheel size, along with the method of operation, could be modified to suit special customer requirements.

The loading platform was provided with a non-slip, expanded metal surface which provided traction for wheeled vehicles or the roller tracks of pallet loaders. Lifting was effected by scissor-type beams operated by two single-acting hydraulic jacks working at 2,000 psi, the platform able to be held at any intermediate height in the overall range, from 19" in the fully down position to 11' 0" above ground level when extended. A feature built into the design was the ability to match the Hylo up with the angle of the aircraft loading door cill, which occurred if the Hylo and aircraft were on differing surfaces, this being achieved by means of hydraulic jacks fitted at each corner which could be compressed or extended as necessary to tilt the Hylo from side to side.

In the self-propelled version hydraulic power was supplied direct from the self-contained engine unit, but the towed version needed to be used in conjunction with a tractor having a take-off point for hydraulic power, therefore for this version the engine unit was replaced by a towbar, hydraulic hose and quick-release couplings. To effect a changeover from self-propulsion to tractor power took just fifteen minutes.

The turning circle of both versions was 50' 0" and separate trailers could be used in conjunction with them to deal with large loads. Irregularities in ground surface, such as potholes up to 3" deep, could be trafficked easily and when carrying 4 tons of freight on a level surface a maximum speed of 10 mph was possible.

Overall statistics of the Hylo Mk 1 loader were:

length (overall chassis)	21' 0"	height (platform lowered)	3' 4"
length (with car ramps extended)	29' 0"	height (platform fully up)	11' 0"
width (chassis)	8' 11"	minimum ground clearance	4"
platform length	16' 6"	turning circle diameter	50' 0"
platform width	6' 9"		

When the Hylo Mk 2 was introduced the power unit for the self-propelled version was changed to a 15 hp Coventry Victor engine which provided the motive power and operated the twin ram-operated scissor lift. As with the Hylo Mk 1, the Mk 2 could be driven at up to 10 mph in forward or reverse gears. For the towed version of the Mk 2 a Lister tug unit was generally used with an articulated link.

During initial performance trials the Hylo was compared with another lift, the four-pillar type manufactured by Littlegreen Engineering, but it was obvious that the Hylo would be more suited to the car-ferry role. The Littlegreen Car-go unit was battery-operated and self-propelled, and with a capacity of 2½ tons could be used more in the pure freight role.

British European Airways tested the Hylo at Southend using one of their Argosy freighters and subsequently ordered a total of seventeen in three different models, these being used in loading large packages up to the size of the International 88" x 108" pallet. Development of the Hylo loaders continued throughout the service life of the ATL98, one version being designed solely to load the 88" x 108" pallet into the Ansett-ANA aircraft.

A later type of scissor lift, produced in 1973 by Houchins of Ashford, Kent, was the Freightmaster 12000. Its name derived from the fact that it could take a full load of 12000 lbs at 8 mph and up a 1:20 gradient. The maximum height achievable was 12' 0" and final platform adjustments could be controlled by the operator using a hand-held remote control system. By 1973 vehicle air ferry operations from Kent had reduced and it was offered for use in the pure freight role, into which market it made a slight inroad but not enough to become a major influence.

The Hylo loader, in this case a Mk 2 self-propelled version for Aer Lingus seen carrying a mixed load of freight.   *(ATEL photo via A.C. Leftley)*

Whilst conversion of G-ANYB was in progress the erstwhile Don Cartlidge carried on with his flying, rather than remain inactive, by getting more types (including the DC4) onto his logbook. Once his employment with Lord Derby was finally terminated he was then asked by Aviation Traders to pay a brief visit to Farnborough on 21 April 1961 where he, as a former graduate of the Empire Test Pilots' School there, took up a Blackburn Beverley for some cross-country flights in order to get used to the height of the cockpit above ground level. In the case of this type the pilot's eye level was at 25' 0" and not dissimilar to that proposed for the ATL98 at 22' 8", so with this new type on his licence Cartlidge was able to face the ATL98 with less trepidation on its first flight exactly two months later.

1961 – First flight and subsequent evaluation

Conversion of G-ANYB progressed until 13 May 1961 when the semi-complete airframe, less engines, outer wing sections and control surfaces, was rolled out of the hangar and into view for the first time. With basic construction now being complete it only remained for the production staff and instrument fitters to finish installation work on the equipment and systems before refitting all the major flight components and control surfaces. All four engines, along with their 3-blade Hamilton Standard propellors, were then refitted and the finished aircraft was moved into the paint shop for spraying in Channel Air Bridge colours.

Whilst the aircraft was finally cleared by Aviation Traders for engine tests and taxi trials on June 20 the Air Registration Board had not given full flight clearance, therefore it was never intended to make any attempts at flight that day. Ground exercises were therefore limited purely to high speed accelerate-stop tests, but as Don Cartlidge, Bob Langley and flight test engineer Ken Smith were carrying out one of the many runs on the runway at Southend in the late afternoon the aircraft became airborne for a short distance before the situation was realised. The aircraft should have been firmly on the ground throughout all the high speed runs but, due to the fact that the aircraft was lightly loaded, the over-extension of the nosewheel meant that Aviation Traders had arrived at a situation which resulted in an increase in the angle of attack of the wing section with the aircraft on the ground. This increase, albeit only one degree above that for the original DC4 design, and the subsequent brief airborne excursion had no ill effects and only served to boost the confidence of the test team, accordingly full preparations were made for the official first flight planned for the following day.

In the early hours of 21 June the aircraft was made ready for its maiden flight, the event being well attended by Freddie Laker and officials from British United, the entire Aviation Traders design team and members of the press. Also eagerly awaiting the results of ten months labour were the production shop workers, who turned out en masse to watch what would be for them an extremely satisfying sight. Led by Don Cartlidge, who always flew in sports jacket and flannels whilst the others used flying suits, the flight test crew boarded the aircraft and commenced pre-start checks.

The engines started smoothly and, with after-start and system checks complete, G-ANYB, wearing the colours and triple arrowhead badge of Channel Air Bridge, taxied out from the apron and was held at the head of Runway 24. After power and magneto checks the brakes were released and, at 0825 hrs, the first of the new generation of vehicle air ferry aircraft was airborne and in its true element.

Once clear of the airport circuit and in cruising trim G-ANYB was joined by a chase plane for the purpose of photography and closer observation. This was a Cessna 310D piloted by another Aviation Traders test pilot, Captain L.P. Griffith, and carrying company directors Charles Murrel and Captain J.R. Batt, plus Chief Designer Arthur Leftley, whose previous worries were now dispelled by the evidence flying before their eyes some yards distant. After formating with the ATL98 for a while the Cessna broke away to return to Southend, leaving the test team to carry on with what was to be a two-hour flight, for now the real testing was just beginning and 'NYB would be undergoing an intensive programme of flight trials before acceptance of certification was obtained from the Air Registration Board.

The semi-finished fuselage of G-ANYB after having been rolled out by musclepower from Aviation Traders' hangar at Southend on 13 May 1961. The refitting of flying surfaces, the engines, equipment and fittings is yet to commence. *(ATEL photo via A.C. Leftley)*

Photographed from the chase plane the first Carvair, G-ANYB, is seen landing on Runway 24 at Southend after the flights of 23 June 1961. Still a very clean aircraft, the individual name and 'Carvair' logo have yet to be painted on the nose. Behind the aircraft is Rochford golf course and the railway line, with the hospital tower in Rochford town prominent in the background. *(Ken Woolcott photo)*

On this first flight the aircraft was flown at a comparatively light weight of 54,000 lbs and a mid-c.g. position. It was taken up to 10,000 feet over the Thames Estuary where cruise checks were made. Following this it was then taken to Vne, at 217 kts, and then down to Vdf, at 97 kts. Two straight stalls in a clean configuration were also carried out with only a 1,000' loss of height and showed no trace of pre-stall buffeting. On return to Southend a total block time of 2 hrs 10 mins was recorded, with exactly two hours being spent on the flying side of the tests, and no changes were deemed necessary at this stage to the aircraft trim, or the engines and systems.

At the end of its first working day the new aircraft was securely tucked away in the 'black hangar' before the usual wining and dining celebrations took place at the Bell hotel on the Southend arterial road, here the success of all those concerned with the project was toasted and the pattern of work for the following day discussed. Tests the next day matched those of the first by way of evaluation and routine checks, but 23 June proved to be more of a trial than any at this early stage. On only the aircraft's fourth flight (the second that day) it was demonstrated to the Permanent Under-Secretary of the Ministry of Aviation. In an attempt to interest the Ministry as to any possible military application it was displayed on the ground and then flown repeatedly up and down the Southend runway for the assembled VIPs, these having been invited to see if the type could have any military usage, but any role other than the task it was designed for never came about.

Note – In this and subsequent chapters details of dates and the precise nature of trials work carried out, as well as all the 'first flights', inaugurals and crew conversion training for customers, are extracted from Don Cartlidge's flight logbook.

Official interest in the ATL98 having now been forgotten the test team continued with the flying programme and busied themselves with air work as time was moving on towards the next milestone, the acceptance test flight for the Air Registration Board inspectors. It must be remembered that the ATL98 was to be compared with the DC4, performancewise, and had to be at least equal but certainly not less than that type. In other words the aircraft was being cleared to DC4 standard.

The aircraft was positioned to Filton on 27 June for calibration trials and pitot position error corrections. These had to be carried out in daylight but early enough to have smooth weather conditions, and as suitable conditions did not occur immediately it took two days to complete these tests before returning to Southend.

The only real problem on the aerodynamic side encountered during the actual test flying was resolved quite early on in the programme and concerned the rudder actions. As noted previously in the chapter dealing with design of the airframe and layout Aviation Traders had, in an attempt to counterbalance the effect of a longer front fuselage, increased the fin area by capping off the top. The resultant shape, not dissimilar to the DC7C, produced a more efficient fin and rudder arrangement such that in the early test flying stages a rudder overbalance condition existed when the aircraft was put into a full sideslip. In order to see aft during tests associated with, particularly, the rudder actions a periscope was fixed into a temporary window in the upper escape hatch. Accessible from the flight deck it was also used to view the wings.

On one occasion in particular, when the test crew were climbing 'NYB out over the Thames Estuary from about 300 feet in the take-off configuration of full power with the flaps and undercarriage extended, full rudder was applied and the fin became fully stalled. On this occasion prestall buffet was also present and of sufficient magnitude to produce a full stall of the whole aircraft, had the situation been allowed to progress further. Recovery action was initiated, namely the immediate centralisation of the rudder controls, and a return to straight flight was attained, but not before many loud bangs had been heard from behind the flight deck. These were caused by the magazine of the F24 camera, fixed to record the automatic observer panel behind the crew seats, coming free from its rubber bungees and striking opposite sides of the fuselage during the prestall buffeting.

The observer panel, photographed at one-minute intervals during flight tests, contained a manifold

The Carvair programme test pilots after the first flights of G-ANYB. Don Cartlidge always flew in shirt and tie whilst Bob Langley was more practically attired, as befitted his earlier vocation as bomber pilot with the Royal Air Force. *(Ken Woolcott photo)*

pressure and rpm gauge (for all engines), a wide scale airspeed indicator, sensitive altimeter, outside air temperature, clock and gallons gone indicator. Outside air temperature was measured by an impact resistant bulb mounted beneath the yaw vane boom at the port wing tip, and additionally the pilot's engine instruments were calibrated, with the captain's standard ASI being replaced by a calibrated wide-scale unit. Three Hussenot A20 flight data recorders were carried, No 1 to cover airspeed, altitude, elevator position and the elevator trim tab position, No 2 covering elevator and aileron stick force, port aileron position and vertical acceleration, and No 3 the port and starboard rudder pedal force, rudder angle and angle of yaw. The latter three transmitters in No 3 also operated indicators which could be seen visually from inside the cockpit.

In the intermediate stage of these tests the rudder travel was reduced from the 20 degrees of the basic C54 to 18 degrees in an attempt towards alleviating rudder overbalance and, after analysis of this particular series of trials and prior to the final assessment of lateral and directional characteristics, a further reduction of 2 degrees was made. A rudder travel of 16 degrees was adopted for the remainder of the flight trials and subsequent production, and was the only change made to the ATL98 design during post-conversion flight trials.

It should be noted that the Decca Flight Log was used during the trials in order to remain within the airspace 'block' allocated to Aviation Traders for test purposes, this being a tiny portion of the congested airspace between two airways, the Shoeburyness danger area and the FIR boundary into Belgian airspace. Channel Air Bridge had previously fitted Decca into all its Bristol Freighters and as a natural progression one was installed in 'NYB. The entire flight trials programme was carried out using this aid, probably the first recorded occasion on which it was used for such a purpose. An autopilot was also fitted for the tests, this being the gyroscopically-controlled Jack and Heintz Type A-3A, which operated the flight controls hydraulically via servo units in the control cable systems. Used on a number of occasions during the flying programme it operated satisfactorily without adjustment.

For a considerable period of time during flight trials the nosewheel undercarriage system presented snags. These first arose due to the continual adjustments having to be made on the ground to the length of the distance piece on the nosewheel actuating jack following the change in geometry of the undercarriage leg travel. During the course of many, sometimes inappropriate, adjustments required to achieve the complete and correct noseleg retraction 'NYB was often seen flying around with its undercarriage in the lowered position until the correct length of distance piece was arrived at.

Another cause of incorrect operation, this time with the nosewheel failing to lower, arose from stretch in the cable which operated the sequence locks and latches. When the control lever was functioned the cable (now in the order of 15' – 20' long) stretched such that the hydraulic selectors came in before the up-lock latches were released, and as the hydraulic pressure built up in the 'down' line it prevented the 'up' locks from being withdrawn. Although the cockpit warning lights gave indications that all the gear was coming down the nosewheel was in fact still retracted. On the number of occasions when Don Cartlidge was only getting two confirmed 'greens' for the main wheels he had to resort to the temporary remedy of retracting the main wheels and then vigorously selecting 'down'. This eliminated a certain amount of stretch in the cable, but until modifications were made to the cable and nosewheel latch adjustment it was often necessary for the on-board engineer to go down to the freight hold and give the offending cable (conveniently labelled in its sidewall location) a hard pull as the pilot selected 'down', in order to free the up-lock latches.

Work continued until the afternoon of 23 July, when an unfortunate setback at Southend halted the flight programme and other trials. Whilst G-ANYB was parked on the tarmac outside Aviation Traders' hangar a company employee driving a fork-lift truck collided with the aircraft, striking the port tailplane leading edge. It was not recorded what happened to the driver but subsequent examination of the aircraft showed the tail section to have been practically severed from the remainder of the rear fuselage.

Port side view of the rear of G-ANYB showing the damage to the fuselage caused when the fork-lift truck hit the port tailplane at Southend Airport.   *(ATEL photo)*

A close-up of the underside of the port tailplane showing the large tear in the fuselage skinning at the tailplane spar on station X953, as well as the bent and displaced front fairing after the whole unit had been pushed rearwards.

(ATEL photo)

At this juncture the flight test programme was unfinished, but had reached a satisfactory and advanced stage, and the damage, whilst substantial, could not warrant writing off the aircraft as it was the 'pattern' for the production line being established at Stansted. As the results from flight trials of the first converted aircraft could have influenced production time and methods it was necessary to complete and assess these before production got too advanced. Thoughts of modifying another C54 aircraft to finish the flight trials were out of the question due to the time involved, therefore repairs were put in hand immediately. The work was carried out with all haste but the enforced grounding occupied a period of good flying weather during the whole of August and September, with the aircraft not being made serviceable and cleared for completion of the post-conversion tests until early October.

With the aircraft once again serviceable, on 8 October the test team again positioned it to Filton where the next series of tests were to assess performance at a maximum T.O.W. of 73,800 lbs. Measured take-offs and landings were the principal order of these tests but in the initial stages it was not possible to achieve this for, after the very first takeoff, the crew were required by law to jettison fuel and water ballast in order to arrive at a reduced landing weight of 64,000 lbs. This was not only time-consuming and costly but also served to defeat the object of a continuous series of trials. Eventually a dispensation was given for the test team to land the aircraft back at 73,800 lbs, less the small amount of fuel actually consumed during the exercise (which only went to a full throttle height of 2000'), provided that the rate of descent on final approach was no more excessive than that of the DC4 with which it was being evaluated.

The test flying at Filton continued until 23 October when the aircraft was flown back to Southend for more detailed work. A return was made to Filton on 30 October which was to last until 23 November. At Southend radio tests were completed on 2 December and all test data was eventually finalised in January 1962. As the date for the acceptance test flight drew nearer, and work intensified, gaps in the flight data filled rapidly. Apart from local flying and trips to Filton excursions were also made to Manston in Kent where a long and extra-wide runway available there was ideal for assymetrical power takeoffs and cross-wind flight conditions.

Whilst the flight test team were becoming extremely confident in the aeroplane one small detail had been overlooked. As noted previously Don Cartlidge had flown a Beverley in order to get used to the pilot's eye height above ground (and wheel) level, but no-one had thought to emphasise this aspect during the testing period. With the pilot's eye in the safe approach slope on a VASI set the ATL98 undercarriage was much lower, and the aircraft would not make the theoretical approach surface. After a reputable witness confirmed that 'NYB had removed the red obstruction lights placed near the pig farm on the approach to Runway 06 at Southend with its wheels, the Southend Airport management checked its VASI geometry, with the result that the VASIs were raised to ensure adequate clearance for the ATL98 over the railway line at the Runway 24 approach, and the pig farm ...

1962 – ups and downs

In preparation for the anticipated sales of their new product the marketing department of Aviation Traders had been working at full speed. Apart from the expected sales to their 'local' airline, Channel Air Bridge, it was hoped that other vehicle-carriers as well as some of the medium-sized airlines would take an interest in the ATL98. The cost for a standard conversion, with ATEL providing the aircraft, was in the order of £160,000 whereas if the customer supplied one of their own aircraft the cost was much lower. If the customer then required the newly-converted aircraft to have its equipment or systems match that of other C54 or DC4 types already in their fleet, or just be fitted out to suit their own particular requirements, the cost varied according to the amount of work involved.

By early 1962 the sales brochure for the ATL98 was complete. As well as all the normal promotional features it highlighted the capability and versatility of the type by giving full weight breakdowns for the three fuselage layouts offered. These breakdowns, relating to the carrying capacity of each layout, are reproduced as Table 2 in their original format but it should be noted that the passenger capacity for the standard vehicle-ferry configuration was given as 20, and not the 23 as generally carried.

Table 2 – Weight breakdown of original three layouts designed

FUSELAGE LAYOUT No 1
Car Ferry – 5 cars and 20 passengers

	lbs	lbs
BASIC AIRCRAFT		
Empty Weight		40,372
Partitions and Decorations	210	
Furnishings and Equipment	247	
Passenger Seats	400	
Passenger Service Items	100	
Car Marshal/Steward	165	
Crew (2)	330	
		1,452
OPERATING EMPTY WEIGHT		41,824
4 Medium Cars		10,400
1 Small Car		1,500
20 Passengers and Baggage		4,000
ZERO FUEL AND OIL WEIGHT (max 59000 lbs)		57,724
Oil	600	
*Fuel	5,172	
		5,772
		63,496

*Range With Fuel = 250 nm (I.F.R.) With Full S.B.A.C. Allowances

Table 2 (continued)

FUSELAGE LAYOUT No 2

32 Passenger – Freighter Version

(Maximum fuel with maximum payload)

	lbs	lbs
BASIC AIRCRAFT		
Empty Weight		40,372
Partitions and Decorations	260	
Furnishings and Equipment	338	
Passenger Seats	800	
Drinking and Washing Water	100	
Passenger Service Items	160	
Crew (2)	330	
Steward	165	
		2,153
OPERATING EMPTY WEIGHT		42,525
32 Passengers and Baggage		6,400
Freight		10,075
MAXIMUM ZERO FUEL AND OIL WEIGHT		59,000
Oil	600	
*Fuel	14,200	
		14,800
MAXIMUM TAKE-OFF WEIGHT		73,800

*Range With Fuel = 1,475 nm   With Full S.B.A.C. Allowances

FUSELAGE LAYOUT No 3

Long Range Freight Version

	lbs	lbs
BASIC AIRCRAFT		
Empty Weight		40,372
Additional Crew Furnishings	228	
Crew (3)	495	
Crew Baggage	120	
Navigator's Equipment	50	
Water	100	
		993
OPERATING EMPTY WEIGHT		41,365
Freight		17,635
ZERO FUEL AND OIL WEIGHT (max 59000 lbs)		59,000
Oil	600	
*Fuel	14,200	
		14,800
MAXIMUM TAKE-OFF WEIGHT		73,800

*Range With Fuel = 1,475 nm (I.F.R.) With Full S.B.A.C. Allowances

On 10 February the critical air test by the Air Registration Board was passed without fault and the full Certificate of Airworthiness issued. Cartlidge then cleared Captains Underhill and Curtis, the first of the Channel Air Bridge crews, to fly the type. The following day, as Cartlidge was checking out Dudley Scorge (already the company DC4 fleet captain and to be the Carvair fleet captain), the number 3 engine failed but the aircraft returned safely to Southend for the unit to be repaired. This was one of the original powerplants fitted, by coincidence, in the same location as the unit that failed during rig tests at Bristol Siddeley.

G-ANYB on the Southend ramp during the early evaluation period. In the background at right is G-APNH, a C54B claimed by Air Charter as a bad debt and shown here in their colours, destined to become Carvair number 11 some 18 months later. Although the two aircraft are parked at different angles the variations in shape and size of the vertical tail surfaces can be seen.

(ATEL photo via Terry Leighton)

Crew conversion resumed on 13 February with training given to Reg Underhill and Tony Weaber, and on this occasion adverse weather at Southend gave the opportunity to divert to Manston for a check on landings with a crosswind component. In the week following the ARB acceptance four of CAB's pilots were cleared to fly the new type, one being Dudley Scorge who would be captain of the first inaugural flight to Ostende on 16 February 1962.

Prior to 'NYB entering company service it had been decided that the new type should not suffer any anonymity in the initial operational period, and accordingly a competition was held to produce a suitable name. The result of this was the name **Carvair**, which was a contraction of the phrase 'car-via-air', and aptly suited the aircraft for the role in which it was intended. Also painted on 'NYB before eventual acceptance by Channel Air Bridge was the individual aircraft name 'Golden Gate Bridge', intended to emphasise the link between the car ferry, or air bridge as it became known, and the Channel crossings. Later aircraft carried different 'bridge' names relating to the various airports the company operated into. 'NYB carried this, the first of these names, when it went into service alongside the ageing Bristol Freighters which were then gradually taken out of operational use by the company.

Before Channel Air Bridge could operate the Carvair on the proposed long-haul services it had been decided to run a proving flight with freight to a distant Continental destination, but this notion was preceded by the first cross-Channel service which went to Ostende on 16 February 1962. On this inaugural flight 'NYB was flown by Dudley Scorge, fleet captain for the new type, with Don Cartlidge as First Officer and included the Swiss Ambassador amongst the distinguished passenger complement. The flight returned that same day and all on board found the flight time of 45 minutes to be a great improvement, both in terms of speed and comfort, over the times previously logged by the Bristol Freighters.

As a trial for the Carvair on the 'deep-penetration' routes to destinations in south-eastern Europe, a flight to Malaga, Spain, was initiated and on 17 February G-ANYB set out from Southend on its first revenue flight. Chartered by Ford (UK) with a full load of new cars for exhibition and sales promotion the passengers included ATEL chief designer Arthur Leftley, with Douglas Wybrew, Harold Godden and Mortimer Jones from the main British United group, Van Lerrup from the Belgian sales office, photographer Guy Craven, plus Cliff Barrett and Dick Worthington from British United Air Ferries.

The flight had planned to return the same day but hit one snag which proved a major one for, whilst taxiing out at Malaga for the flight home, one hydraulic pump failed. Although the flight could have been accomplished with the remaining equipment functioning perfectly the captain, again Dudley Scorge, opted to cancel the take-off and have the pump repaired. His decision was upheld and arrangements were made for repairs to the failed unit, but for the passengers, travelling for enthusiastic as well as technical reasons, the outcome was an unexpected stopover in Spain. Facilities at Malaga were somewhat lacking to the extent that it was even necessary to manhandle 'NYB around on the tarmac, but eventually the pump was repaired and the aircraft returned to Southend on 19 February to unload its quota of red-faced passengers, none of whom had been prepared for a two night stopover by way of luggage or foreign currency.

Upon return to Southend 'NYB was put in for a thorough service check, before the vital crew training was able to recommence on 28 February with Henry Hartley being cleared for the type. The inaugural flight to Rotterdam was flown on 3 March by Don Cartlidge with Bob Langley as First Officer, and the following day Cartlidge again visited Manston when he cleared Captain John Toothill during crew conversion. Toothill was later to die at Rotterdam as a result of the first accident to a Carvair in service.

A flight to Geneva on 11 March for route proving was captained by Bob Langley with Don Cartlidge as First Officer, and on 17/18 March Rotterdam was scheduled four times, as the rate of usage on the Continental routes swiftly built up. Cartlidge had by now been loaned to Channel Air Bridge for crew line training, as well as being available to flight-test each new aircraft as it came off the production line at Stansted.

Stansted production

In parallel with the post-conversion evaluation of G-ANYB arrangements for a production line at Stansted were being finalised. Having insufficient space at Southend, plus the lack of adequate facilities in the 'black hangar', the decision to place the production line at Stansted was an obvious one as it was already the company's main engineering base.

In readiness for the forthcoming conversion operations Aviation Traders started to gather the various aircraft together at Stansted, this being the final destination for the C54 and later DC4 types ferried into the United Kingdom. After each incoming flight had cleared customs at Southend a steady, if not slightly irregular, stream of C54 types arrived at the parking base adjacent to Hangar 1 where they awaited their turn to enter the production line. On various occasions throughout the programme an aircraft would arrive, sometimes rather clandestinely in view of the rather dilapidated state of particular acquisitions, but every one was eagerly awaited following the lengthy boardroom wranglings over the cost of the work to be done.

During the early stages of the production line being set up, the greatest number of aircraft awaiting conversion to ATL98 were amassed there by ATEL than later on when the stream had slowed down somewhat to the extent that months (and in some cases, years) elapsed between each delivery and the subsequent commencement of work on each one.

The centre of operations was Hangar 1, owned by ATEL, and here the first three airframes to arrive at Stansted in the same time period were put on the production line in the latter part of 1961. These were G-ARSD, 'RSF and 'RSH, all C54 types, with work commencing on the 18th, 22nd and 27th July respectively. These were the first of twenty subsequently converted, although two were later produced at Southend in 1965 and 1968, and as with all those awaiting work at Stansted were kept in open storage until required.

Draining off the fuel tank contents was a prior requisite to removing the wing sections outboard of the engines, also the fin, rudder and tailplane components, for even the choice of Stansted had its space problems. In order to get the aircraft into a T2 hangar with an internal width of 114' 0", compared with the C54 wingspan of 117' 6", it was necessary to remove these items. When these preliminary operations were finished the C54 fuselages, still complete with engines, were tractor-towed along the public road which ran past one end of the hangar and inside to the positions allocated for work to commence. Once inside the first job was to position the fuselages across the width, the floor area being divided up into widthwise bays, and level up each one in turn onto trestles. It was thus possible to accommodate three de-tipped aircraft in the hangar at any one time for the next stage, the removal of engines and the original nose section forward of the wings.

After disconnection of primary controls and other services passing rearwards through the structure the original nose was removed in exactly the same manner as G-ANYB, namely by cutting through the fuselage stringers in a stepped line from fuselage station X360 at the top and forward to station X270 at the bottom. The skinning in the joint area was then unfastened and peeled back for access, the cut stringer ends were cleaned up and the open fuselage lined up and braced in position ready for installation of the new front fuselage.

The first three Carvairs on the Stansted production line, showing G-ARSF (No 3) with work centred on the connection of the front fuselage unit to the main fuselage. Although construction work is not yet complete, masking of the fuselage cheat line for spraying is under way. G-ARSD (No 2) in the background is in a more advanced state. Wing flaps are being worked on in the foreground. At right can be seen the inner starboard mainplane of G-ARSH (No 4) still without its front fuselage unit, as this was having the door opening widened for the forthcoming UN contract, but with a jury frame installed to keep the cut stringer ends in place. (ATEL photo via A.C. Leftley)

In contrast with the building of the first ATL98 completely at Southend only the new front fuselages and ancillary components for production aircraft were manufactured there. Neither Stansted nor Southend could offer space for a complete production line, and additionally in 1961 Aviation Traders also had insufficient space at Southend for parking the aircraft due in for modification, therefore they only remained for a brief period before being flown on to Stansted. Consequently the area where G-ANYB was converted was turned over entirely to the manufacture of scratch-built front fuselages, and although a total of 22 were built only 20 were fitted to production aircraft.

Other production items such as door parts, cills, furnishings, etc, were also produced at Southend and shipped by road to Stansted for installation. The new front fuselages were shipped on a specially-built road trailer and when on the trailer the load was 19' 6" high, the haulage route having to be carefully planned to avoid low bridges and other obstacles.

Whilst the new front fuselages were supposedly ready to be put directly onto a prepared fuselage there were still some snags which arose in the mating process. Although they had a vertically cut rear end and the stringers left slightly over-length, when finally offered up into position a fair amount of joggling of stringers was necessary due to the variations in location arising from components produced in two different places as well as those due to movement of the frames during the road journey to Stansted.

Front fuselages arrived at Stansted complete with primary controls, plus the cockpit glazing refitted to the new profile, but without any nosewheel gear as the pickup points for this were used in securing the unit onto the trailer and also during the handling by crane when lifting and positioning it for fitting onto the rear fuselage. The nose landing gear and the nose loading door were fitted at Stansted once the mating operation was complete and the new front fuselage securely fixed to the fuselage.

(ATEL photo via Dick Worthington)

After fitting each front fuselage unit and splicing the fuselage stringers on both sides of the joint there still remained an amount of fairing-in to be done on the fuselage where the humped top line flowed down to join the original cross-section at the new frame X360. The main problem was that each panel of the new fuselage skin in the joint area had to be put through a double curvature without stressing it too much, and as each aircraft was built more or less individually the same problems recurred each time. All the curved panel work was produced on the same wheeling horse as used for G-ANYB, the first conversion. Either side of the frame at station X360 half frames were added in order to give support strength to the skinning, these being more or less the same for each aircraft, but in cases where types were produced with a different system of controls slight variations existed in the way the pickup points for the pulley rails were fitted on these frames.

Reuse of the original cockpit glazing was considered essential due to the rigid construction schedule and the relative non-availability of windscreens during the initial production period and, until the supply problem was resolved, each windscreen was modified to fit into a new wider surround. The time taken to produce each new layout however proved to be much longer than expected and it was decided to acquire at least one more complete windscreen, albeit possibly still attached to an airframe.

A fuselage was located with KLM at Schipol and approaches made for its purchase, but as the reason for its need was now apparent from articles in the aviation press the sale price was set rather high. Nevertheless, as the spare glazing had to be obtained from somewhere in order to keep ahead at all times with this item, the fuselage was purchased and duly shipped to England for removal of the parts required by ATEL. They were subsequently able to remove a screen from an aircraft in for conversion and replace it with the spare modified item while the original one was modified ready for a following aircraft.

Eventually ATEL were fortunate enough to obtain a large quantity of C54 spares, including the much sought-after windscreens and framing, which eased the demand on modified components for the production line aircraft to the extent such that a reserve stock was built up.

The retention and reuse of original items from aircraft went as far as the control columns and rudder pedals, centre pedestals, seats and the like, all of which were highly tooled components that ATEL were not prepared to set up a production line for, time again being the critical factor.

The time taken to produce each conversion varied according to the 'standardisation' work required, which meant that the customer supplying the aircraft was short in its fleet by that one for a considerable time. In most cases the customer was expected to wait for his own airframe to be converted, which in the meantime could have been earning revenue, and because of this unknown time factor it was suggested that if his aircraft went onto the line and he accepted the next available Carvair from the other end – i.e. some other airframe – the delivery period, and hence the out-of-service time, might be a few weeks shorter.

It would be expected that once production methods had been established and experience was gained conversion time per airframe would reduce, and although the last four aircraft were turned round in roughly four months this was not the norm. The conversion period varied due to the need to produce a 'standard' Carvair, or where a customer required those in the same company fleet to be converted to the same specification. It should also be noted that some conversion periods shown in Table 3 are lengthy, namely for Carvairs 11, 15 and 17 where production was delayed due either to lack of parts or a future customer.

The extension to vertical fin surfaces presented no production continuity problems as all the aeroplanes had the same profile added to existing fittings. In all cases the rear fuselage had strengthened frames and modified rudder fittings installed to cater for the increased size of fin and rudder, and while work in this area was in progress a steel A-frame was attached to the horizontal tail surface pickup points to hold the extreme rear end steady.

Table 3 – Conversion periods for ATL98 aircraft

Carvair	Registration	Douglas type	Conversion period and notes		Conversion duration (months)
1	G-ANYB	C54B	1.10.60 - 21. 6.61	(Southend)	8½
2	G-ARSD	C54A	18. 7.61 - 25. 3.62	(Stansted)	8
3	G-ARSF	C54B	22. 7.61 - 28. 6.62	"	11
4	G-ARSH	C54A	27. 7.61 - 5. 9.62	"	13
5	G-AREK	C54A	27.12.61 - 2.11.62	"	10
6	G-ARZV	C54A	14. 6.62 - 20.12.62	"	6
7	LX-BNG	C54A	17. 8.62 - 19. 3.63	"	7
8	EI-AMR	C54B	23.10.62 - 19. 4.63	"	6
9	G-ASHZ.	C54B	29.10.62 - 8. 6.63	"	7
10	LX-BBP	C54A	11.12.62 - 27. 9.63	"	9½
11	G-APNH	C54B	1.12.62 - 4. 1.65	(Southend)	25
12	G-AOFW	C54A	23. 4.63 - 11. 2.64	(Stansted)	9½
13	G-ASKN	C54A	25. 7.63 - 8. 2.64	"	7½
14	G-ASKD	C54B	31. 7.63 - 17. 4.64	"	8½
15	G-ATRV	C54E	8.11.63 - 23. 3.66	"	28½
16	EC-AEP	C54B	18. 2.64 - 4. 6.64	"	3½
17	G-AXAI	C54B	10. 2.64 - 2. 4.69	"	62
18	EC-AEO	C54B	5.11.64 - 12. 3.65	"	4
19	VH-INJ	DC4	17. 5.65 - 14. 9.65	"	4
20	VH-INK	DC4	26. 6.65 - 27.10.65	"	4
21	VH-INM	C54E	1. 3.68 - 12. 7.68	(Southend)	4½

(These production periods are included in the complete listing of aircraft for the Carvair programme as given in Appendix 6)

During final assembly of components at the tail end of the fuselage a further minor snag arose in some instances concerning the tail cone. For the C54 series there existed two types of tail cone, one being lightweight in construction and fixing, the other of a much heavier nature and fixed with a ring of bolts. The heavier type was intended to be fitted when the C54 was used for towing gliders, hence the stronger material and method of fixing. With these small items there was an obvious weight difference and due to the position in which they were fixed, extremely remote from the aircraft's centre of gravity, it was desirable to refit the lighter type. On some conversions it was necessary to initiate a search for the lightweight version in order to effect a saving in weight.

Another weight-saving exercise carried out by the ATEL production staff was the removal of the heavy pickup points installed in the wings of some C54 variants between the inboard engines and fuselage. These heavy points, accessible from the underside of the wing, were provided in the original Douglas design for the transport of outsize items that could not go inside the fuselage. Items of equipment such as jeeps, large field guns and spare propellers were among those envisaged as travelling 'underwing' by this method, but another use for the heavy points was made by G-ANYB earlier in its life when operating out of La Paz in Bolivia. Due to the altitude there the rarified atmosphere had an undesirable effect on the performance of the R2000 engines fitted and, to overcome this problem and assist with heavily-loaded take-offs, RATOG was installed under the wings. When 'NYB was sold off and operated elsewhere the RATOG system was removed but the heavy points remained.

One point of extreme concern during the production period was the differences in fuselage length, by up to 3" from the standard 94' 10¼", between those aircraft built originally at Orlando and those at Chicago. Aircraft from either facility were identifiable by the addition of a suffix to the type number, the Douglas main factory at Chicago using 'DC' and their facility at Orlando in central Florida employing the letters 'DO'. After working on models from both factories ATEL were able to overcome most of the problems associated with the length differences but the item that produced most variations and holdups in this respect was the installation of the additional emergency exits required by the ARB. As a result of the length differences the spacing between fuselage frames in the new rear passenger cabin varied with each aircraft, sometimes by up to one inch, and affected the whole door frame structure to the extent that each one had to be modelled separately. This of course threw production time out as each exit became an individual job rather than a production item.

Fabrication of the new floor panels was also affected by the fuselage length differences for, although the original corrugated metal flooring was discarded in favour of loose, easily removable sections, these had to be individually made to fit in with the variations in frame and support beam position. Hence each panel was intended only for a particular location and had easy-reference numbers marked on the underside for positioning purposes.

When G-ANYB was converted at Southend the length differences, plus the time involved in dealing with them, were not anticipated and other snags encountered were considered only relative to the prototype. With the production line underway the problem was made worse when companies supplied different aircraft marks and required them to be converted to the same standard, thus production times varied even for aircraft of the same sub-type.

The rear fuselages of the first three Carvairs on the Stansted production line, showing on G-ARSH the original operation of the rear entry doors. In 'bridge' use the rear half was fixed shut. Even though 'RSH, and 'RSD at rear, were both C54A-10-DC sub-types from the main factory, variations can be seen in the size and position of the rear windows, whilst a different window layout exists for 'RSF (a C54B-5-DO from Orlando) in the centre.   *(ATEL photo via Terry Leighton)*

A non-structural revision made to the basic C54 design as part of the conversion was to fix the rear half of the rear loading door in the closed position. This was held shut with steel plates while the forward half was used as before for passenger entry.

Generally the usual snags encountered during each conversion arose from the operations necessary in modifying the fuel system, both in the matter of installing the complicated runs of operating cables in the new front fuselage and in the use and repositioning of the various valves and associated fittings in the wings.

With the much longer cables employed, and the number of changes in direction realised, a large amount of cable stretch was encountered, with the consequence that obtaining full and free operation of fuel valves between the 'open' and 'closed' positions occupied quite a time in the fitting stage. In respect of this, and all the cable-operated controls, periodic checks and adjustments were necessary in order to maintain the correct overall cable tension for each circuit, bearing in mind the effect of numerous pulleys at various positions along the run. Tensiometer readings were taken at set locations on each circuit and adjustments made as required on this basis.

The main problem with the fuel systems was that aircraft under conversion were different marks of the C54 design, either 'A', 'B' or 'E', and consequently had differing locations on the wing spars for the fuel lines and valves. Some aircraft had also been further modified in some way or another by previous operators. The C54 'A' and 'B' types originally had a front spar system whereby all the fuel system fittings were mounted on the front wing spar, but when in use with the United States Air Force were converted to have eight tanks and a rear spar system. These variations produced the C54G and also applied to certain DC4 types, but when conversion work was underway on some of the earlier aircraft it was found these had very makeshift systems with some fittings having been left on the front spar and others completely changed to have a rear spar system or a combination of each.

The basic C54A had four integral fuel tanks in the fuselage with 'dry' outer wing sections, although when aeroplanes of this type were in service and engaged on long-range freight and trooping runs with the air transport divisions of the USAF a further four round tanks were mounted in the fuselage. The C54B had only two integral fuselage tanks but carried additional tankage in the form of 'wet' outer wing sections. For eight-tank versions, of the C54G type generally, flexible 'bag' tanks were also fitted in the wings between the fuselage and inboard engines.

The Carvair fuel system was based on a direct adoption of the front spar system for the C54A and it would, therefore, have appeared to have been merely the case for a relatively simple overhaul operation, but as some aeroplanes came in for conversion as eight-tank or six-tank versions and the fuel valves for these systems differed anyway, all the valves and mounting brackets had to be changed for the required layout which in turn meant each fuel system had to be modelled separately.

With the new front fuselage fixed on, all fuselage systems installed and the work associated with the wing-mounted systems complete (this being the most time-consuming item) each aircraft was then turned through 90 degrees in preparation to exit the production line. The outer wing sections were then refitted in the hangar but the 48" wide wing-tip sections had to wait until the aircraft was outside as the hangar width would not allow this.

1962 – ups and downs in service

Production at Stansted had now caught up after the earlier delivery of G-ANYB and the second Carvair, G-ARSD, fully modified as a result of what few changes eminated from the test flying of 'NYB, was first flown at 1927 hrs on Sunday, 25 March. However on this flight so many faults arose with the aircraft and systems it was decided to fly it direct to Southend for immediate repairs. It was now a race against time to get ready for the ARB clearance flights, required to establish that the second and subsequent aircraft were to the same standard as the first, so that production could continue unhindered. On 28 March, after being worked on in the hangar for three days, 'RSD was once again serviceable and then underwent nine hours and thirty minutes of exhaustive test flying spread over four days. Apart from problems associated with fuel dumping all snags were cleared, and on 31 March Don Cartlidge flew it with the two ARB assessors on board to enable the ATL98 to be fully cleared. Although smooth and satisfactory fuel dumping was a problem that existed throughout the programme this was a DC4 snag, and not specific to the Carvair.

G-ARSD was handed over to Channel Air Bridge on 2 April with the name 'Chelsea Bridge' just in time for the inaugural flight on the deep-penetration service to Geneva that same day. To say that things were cut a bit fine is not an understatement, for the Certificate of Airworthiness only arrived at the aircraft by motor-cycle courier five minutes before takeoff!

In August of the previous year Channel Air Bridge had been granted a licence to operate a Carvair service on the Southend-Basle route, as well as to Strasbourg and Geneva, and with G-ARSD now available the intention was to fly all the inaugural flights on the 'deep-penetration' routes using both aircraft delivered up at this time. For the run to Geneva Bob Langley flew the press contingent in 'NYB while Don Cartlidge carried passengers in 'RSD on a parallel course with a 15 minute separation. The first of the scheduled Geneva services went out on 5 April. Both aircraft then carried cars when they went to Basle on 6 April using a similar flight plan to the Geneva run and on 31 May, but only using 'NYB to take out Freddie Laker, Douglas Wybrow and the press, for the inaugural to Strasbourg which returned on 3 June.

On 28 June, just three months after 'RSD first flew, the third Carvair took to the air over Stansted. As the second aircraft to have been bought in very bad condition from somewhat doubtful dealers in the United States, much more work was needed for a finally converted state to be achieved, but after eight hours and thirty minutes on test spread over many days it was handed over to Channel Air Bridge at Southend on 7 July with the registration G-ARSF and the name 'Pont de L'Europe'. The aircraft's C of A documents were issued at Southend just hours before its first service flight to Genoa at 0845 hrs that same day.

G-ARSF outside the British United hangar at Southend shortly after its entry into service with Channel Air Bridge.   *(ATEL photo via Terry Leighton)*

On 16 July 1962, six months after receiving its first new car ferry aircraft, Channel Air Bridge left the main British United group and became a separate air ferry unit with the name of British United Air Ferries. Although having left the company group it had been associated with, including the recently-acquired Silver City Airways, the ideals and lines of operation remained the same. The only noticeable change was in the aircraft livery where 'British United' replaced 'Channel Air Bridge' on the fuselage sides, and 'British United Air Ferries' appeared in full across the top of the fuselage nose loading door opening so as to be visible during loading. The 'bridge' names were retained by the new company.

When each newly-converted aircraft left the Stansted production line it carried the colour scheme and any insignia of the new operator. With very few exceptions all the artwork and individual company markings were hand applied by one man, Reg Taylor, who had carried out scheme painting work with ATEL since the earlier days of the Accountant project.

Companies generally specified how their aircraft were to be finished but once the basic idea had been agreed artwork details were left to the signwriter to finalise. As part of the sales drive to sell conversions ATEL produced an advertisement for the aviation press which showed side elevations of Carvairs already ordered, and finished in the colour schemes of various companies. As some conversions had not been painted by the time the advertisement appeared it employed a certain amount of artistic licence and although reasonably accurate varied just slightly from the final layout. All schemes were generally similar in that they were based on the use of a full length fuselage cheat line which ran either to the tail cone or swept up the fin sides.

In the month following its delivery into service G-ARSF was captained by Don Cartlidge on many cross-Channel flights, and was used by Don and Bob Langley for the first scheduled Carvair flight into Calais on 7 August. Calais was a much smaller airport than others on the vehicle ferry routes but on this occasion, and subsequently, the type coped well.

All the important first flights on the European routes were interspersed with the vital crew training necessary to convert CAB flight crews onto the new type, on which Cartlidge was constantly busy but managed to clear each 'student' in the required time. Much of the crew training was carried out on the short cross-Channel routes, where the crew benefitted from closer intervals between take-off and landing than on the longer 'deep-penetration' services.

Aviation Traders' production rate had now increased to the point where, in the eighteen months after delivery of the first Carvair to Channel Air Bridge, nine aircraft passed out of Stansted for delivery to British United Air Ferries and other users. One such was No 4, previously G-ARSH, first flown on 5 September 1962 bearing the Class B markings of G-41-2 as its first Carvair registration. This was applied to the unsold aircraft for a short period after conversion until such time as a new operator took ownership and the country of registry was determined. Aviation Traders had only once before had cause to apply this system of numbering, the previous occasion being on their other own-design the ATL90 Accountant, another idea from the Laker stable. This too had been without a registration until painted as G-41-1, but then became appropriately G-ATEL for the 1957 SBAC air display at Farnborough.

G-ARSH was the third of the earlier acquisitions purchased by Channel Air Bridge from the American company of Resort Airlines Incorporated in July 1961, after being declared surplus to requirements following the completion of a long-term military freight-carrying contract. 'RSH, along with 'RSD and 'RSF, had then been taken out of service and put into open storage at Oakland, California, before being sold and ferried to Stansted. Channel Air Bridge obtained a fourth from the same source when 'RZV arrived a year later.

After three test flights on 5 September for certification work G-ARSH was then bought by Intercontinental (U.S.) Incorporated, and when handed over on 24 September carried the American registration N9758F. Between these dates Cartlidge and Langley used it to carry out crew training on the type for three pilots from Interocean Airways S.A., a subsidiary of Intercontinental (U.S.) who operated a freight carrier service based in Luxembourg, as Interocean crews were soon to fly the aircraft on lease to the United Nations Organisation for ferrying essential supplies into the troubled Belgian Congo. For this lease it carried the French titles 'Organisations des Nations Unies au Congo' in black on the white fuselage topsides, to avoid any possibility of the operators' identity being misinterpreted. The only colour trim was a 2" deep black cheat line, whilst on the bare metal undersides beneath the nose the initial letters ONUC were prominently displayed, also in black.

N9758F was modified whilst on the Stansted production line to have the front loading door aperture reshaped to allow the carriage of lightweight trucks specified as the principal item of freight for the U.N. charter. The door threshold was widened and strengthened, with cutouts stiffened by stainless steel doublers and strap plates added to the top corners of the opening, and the door lock units repositioned lower down on the frames.

A Bedford truck of the type specified for carriage during the UN charter being loaded into N9758F on 15 September 1962, with the driver just about to duck down before entering the hold. The white label on the vertical edge of the door bottom was applicable only to Carvairs on the UN contract (using the portable loading ramps) and read: 'door warning – to avoid damage to freight door, ramp pickup bars must be positioned inboard before closing'. In the nose loading door is the portable toilet with its privacy curtain.   (ATEL photo via Terry Leighton)

In order for Interocean to gain the U.N. contract loading tests were carried out by ATEL at Southend with N9758F, and a 3½-ton Bedford truck of the type specified, one being borrowed from the Army Garrison at Shoeburyness and stripped down as if for shipment. The cab and body hoops were removed, as were the road wheels which were replaced by smaller wooden service wheels, in order to give the necessary clearance. For the trials it was loaded into the freight hold from a specially-designed wire-braced steel angle section ramp, aided by a winch to drag it into the hold (watched anxiously by its Army owners!). Manual loading however, without the use of a winch, was just possible in the small amount of side space remaining between the truck and aircraft sidewall. As it was not considered practical to employ a standard Hylo lift whilst out in the Congo it was decided to supply a wire-braced ramp which would be shipped out in a dismantled state on the outward flight, then re-assembled at the operating base.

The tests proved successful and on the strength of this the contract was signed but, whilst vehicles of the type trialled could be uplifted, when the modified aircraft flew out to the Congo it was found that the trucks already out there were of the same pattern but slightly different in that the cab was non-removable and the body hoops welded on. These details thus made them impossible to load into the hold, as a result of which the aircraft never carried the type of cargo which was the sole reason for the modifications.

The next Carvair produced was the second of four to have been owned by Air Charter Ltd during the conversion period which flew on 2 November as G-AREK, but was then sold to Intercontinental (U.S.) Incorporated and re-registered as N9757F. This apparently out-of-sequence numbering relates to all United States registered aircraft maintained abroad being given their serial issue in reverse order, the system having started in 1950 with N9999F. After receiving the same modifications as N9758F both aircraft were then transferred over to Interocean Airways S.A, N9757F becoming LX-IOG on 5 December and N9758F taking up LX-IOH oɪɪ the 18th, as they were now under Luxembourg registry.

Bob Langley, Aviation Traders' deputy test pilot, ground-testing the portable toilet in the nose of N9758F, the first Carvair converted for the United Nations contract. (Don Cartlidge photo)

When modified for Interocean use N9758F and '57F were intended from the outset to be operated by a crew of three and, in order to reduce crew fatigue on the anticipated longer all-freight routes, two rest bunks were fitted at the aft end of the flight deck on the port side. Although these rest facilities were provided on the flight deck no galley or toilet was included anywhere in the fuselage, for the addition of even such a small compartment for these would have infringed into the freight area enough to cause a significant reduction in the volume of freight carried. For the relief of crew members a chemical toilet of the Elsan type was fitted on the ledge inside the nose door, this precarious and noisy location being provided with a curtain for the privacy of the occupant.

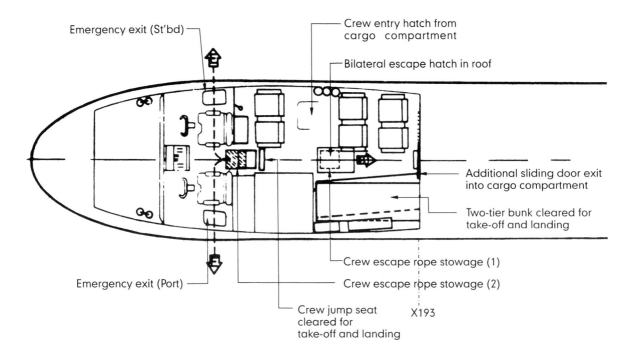

FIGURE 9

Another modification employed on only the Interocean Carvairs was the mounting in the flight deck ceiling of a periscopic sextant. This was fitted to aid navigation on some of the longer routes over which the company would be operating, especially those likely to involve crossings of the Sahara Desert and into Africa. It was also necessary to include a full-time navigator as the third crew member on these long-haul freight runs for this very reason.

After carrying only conventional freight while in the Congo for some two months both the aircraft returned to Southend for servicing and, following a request from Gerry Morris, chief pilot of Interocean, Don Cartlidge and Ken Smith went out to bring LX-IOG back via Leopoldville, Karno, Tripoli and Luxembourg. Apart from converting vehicle-ferry crews onto the new type Cartlidge also ran the odd 'errand' for operators, as well as assisting on the sales side, and this role was to continue for some two years until his departure for a new post with Shannonair.

At the end of December 1962 the Carvair population was up by one then down again, for when No. 6 flew successfully on the 21st and, although still owned by Channel Air Bridge, went straight into service in BUAF colours as G-ARZV, only a week was to pass before G-ARSF crashed in Holland after a new life of just six months.

On 28 December at 1100 hrs GMT G-ARSF was on a scheduled flight into Rotterdam's Zestienhoven Airport with fourteen passengers and four cars when, on approach to runway 24, visibility was impaired by falling snow. The pilot, misjudging the final stages in near white-out conditions, came below the normal glide path and the aircraft struck a six-foot high perimeter dyke at a point some 800 feet short of the runway threshold. The airport runway and approach lighting was on full intensity at

AND 17 GOT OUT ALIVE

Upturned plane pilot dies

By CHRISTOPHER MORRIS

SEVENTEEN people got out alive from this wrecked plane yesterday.

The 14 passengers crawled out without a scratch.

They had been suspended upside down by their belts as the DC3 Dakota lay partly wrecked across a field.

It nose-dived in mud and snow without an engine and with a wing ripped off.

Leak...

Then it hit a dyke and overturned at Zest tenhoven airport, near Rotterdam.

It settled in snow which is believed to have prevented leaking petrol from catching fire.

The pilot, Capt. John Tomlin and First Officer Ron Kitchers were trapped.

An hour's work was needed to free them and Capt. Tomlin aged 35 died on the way to hospital.

The news work was broken to his wife at their home in Hillcrest-road Camberley last night.

He was father of two children and joined the British United Airways from four years ago.

First Officer Kitchers of St. John's avenue, Peters, is in hospital.

A baby

The two other members of the crew, who had slight injuries, were the stewardess Kate Wood aged 24, and air engineer Kenneth Alexander aged 25.

Among the passengers was John Barlow aged 32 of Guildford-road Sussex.

Mr. Barlow's wife Audrey aged 33 is expecting her first baby in three weeks.

Among the passengers flying from Southend were Vicki Caroline Hudson aged seven and her three-year-old sister Ann.

Their father Mr. William Hudson, of Leeds said: The stewardess directed us all to a rope ladder.

Leak...

Then it hit a dyke and overturned at Zest tenhoven airport, near Rotterdam.

It settled in snow which is believed to have prevented leaking petrol from catching fire.

The pilot, Capt. John Tomlin...

The Daily Sketch article on the accident to G-ARSF at Rotterdam on 28 December 1962. The gaping hole left by the missing starboard wing is apparent in the picture, as is the crushed state of the cockpit area which led to the death of the aircraft commander.

47

this time, as the clear visibility in the snow showers was down to 1,600 yards, and the pilot was making a visual approach onto a runway 4,660 feet in length. As G-ARSF came onto finals the runway markers were then partially covered by snow and the whole area local to the airport appeared as one surface.

Full flap was applied when some distance from the runway, as a result of which the rate of descent was too high in relation to the distance left to run onto the runway, and at a high vertical speed the aircraft hit the dyke with its undercarriage before bouncing back into the air and striking the ground 200 feet further on. At this point the complete starboard wing broke away from the fuselage which rolled to the right and slid inverted for some 700 feet before coming to rest, still pointing in the original direction of travel but upside down in a bank of thick snow. The snowbank absorbed leaking aviation spirit from the ruptured wing tanks and prevented it igniting, which was of assistance to the emergency services when they arrived on the scene minutes later.

When the crew were rescued from the crushed flight deck area the pilot's only thought was for the safety of the passengers, but the stewardess later stated that on entering the rear cabin they were all found to be perfectly safe, albeit suspended from their seats by the seat belts. After helping the passengers down from their seats exit was made using the escape rope ladders, and after completing medical checks they carried on their journey in hire cars provided by the airline. The flight crew were taken to hospital and, with the exception of the co-pilot who was detained with shock and the aircraft commander who had died of his injuries during the ambulance journey, all returned to the airport after treatment.

When rescue teams broke into the freight hold all four cars were found to be only slightly damaged and still hanging from the freight floor by the lashing straps, but their removal from the aircraft proved to be quite an exercise. It can only be assumed they were not drivable, due to damage to bodywork and the suspension systems (the lashing points) plus oil flooding from the engines and fluid from the inverted batteries.

Officials from British United Airways flew to Rotterdam for the enquiry, which caused no setbacks in production or delivery of future conversions as the accident was attributed to pilot error under difficult weather conditions prevailing at the time. G-ARSF, still wearing the colours of Channel Air Bridge at the time of the accident, was taken off the British Civil Register on 5 February 1963 just seven months after its new lease of life began. The wreck was purchased from the insurance company and on 23 February shipped from the crash site back to Southend, then to Stansted the following month. Here it was 'stored' outside Hangar No 1 while Aviation Traders stripped all usable parts and consigned what remained to the company's melting pot adjacent to that hangar.

1963 – more over-water routes

After much planning Aer Lingus, the Irish International airline, had announced in February 1963 details of a fourth vehicle-ferry service to be covered by the Carvairs it was to buy. This would start on 20 June and link Dublin direct with Cherbourg, the three other routes already scheduled as due to start on 8 May being Dublin to Liverpool, Dublin to Bristol and Cork to Bristol. All these services were initially once-weekly but once well established the frequency was to be increased, particularly in the case of the most popular route from Dublin to Liverpool which was planned to increase to thirteen per week.

In order to get the new services running G-ARZV was sold by BUAF to Aer Lingus and became the first Carvair on the Irish Register, but although it had first flown in a BUAF scheme was then reconfigured to suit Aer Lingus requirements. For all those delivered to Aer Lingus only 22 seats were fitted in the rear cabin with a further 12 in a new forward cabin in place of the rearmost vehicle space, the number of cars being reduced to four. The original bulkhead at station X758 remained and a new one, with access to the freight hold, was installed at station X600. The rear passenger cabin

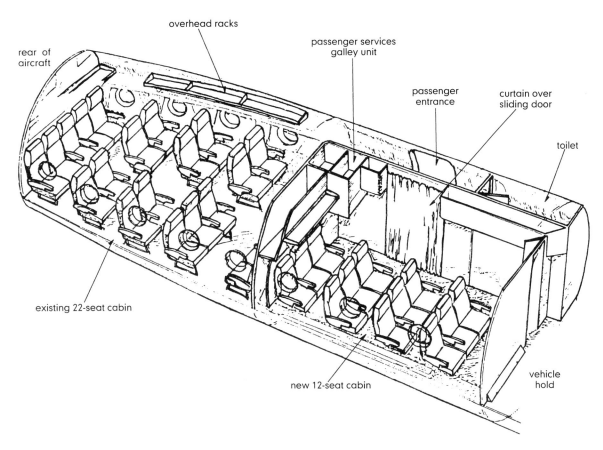

FIGURE 10 – Aer Lingus cabin layout

configuration of 23 seats was used by most aircraft operating in the vehicle-ferry role, but in the case of Aer Lingus the seating capacity was increased to 34 with entry to the new front seating area being by way of the original door into what had been the rear of the freight hold.

The second 'first' flight of 'RZV on 26 February was later than planned due to it having originally been built as a C54A with four wing tanks and 'dry' outer wings and, being required to be to the same specification as the DC4 types operated by the company, many changes had to be made to the fuel system and fittings as well as the installation of further tankage in the outboard wing cells. In addition a Collins 105 flight director was installed, to match similar equipment already fitted to the Aer Lingus Viscount fleet.

Painted in its new livery 'RZV became EI-AMP and carried a Winchester Green fuselage cheat line with white topsides, polished natural aluminium undersides and the company name 'Aer Lingus Irish International' beneath the cockpit, the first two words being in Winchester Green and the last two in a lighter colour known as Dulux Special Green. With a shamrock emblazoned across the vertical tail surfaces the Irish tricolour in green, white and orange (green forward) was carried on the underside of the nose adjacent to the nose-wheel doors, the last two letters of the aircraft registration being repeated on these as per British aircraft. Also painted in Winchester Green beneath the cockpit was the individual aircraft name, EI-AMP being given the name 'Ailbhe', or St Albert, this being in English on the port side and Gaelic on the starboard.

Decor for the cabins was similar to, if not the same as, that for BUAF, namely deep blue carpets and kickstrips with lower wall trims in coral-coloured Vynide and upper walls in white Vynide. Room trim was in gold-starred white Lionide with blue and gold seat covers and plain white satin window curtains. The only obvious change on the Aer Lingus aircraft was that the internal window surrounds were in white, not gold as in the BUAF scheme.

49

On 1 March EI-AMP was flown to Boscombe Down by Don Cartlidge for compass checks, as the remote type required by Aer Lingus needed a more precise compass base than that available at Stansted where the P12 type used by BUAF was checked. Once this was done, and crew training completed, it was flown to Dublin on 13 March and put into service with Cartlidge again acting in the role of training captain during the early operating period.

On 19 March the seventh Carvair flew. This was converted while still owned by Interocean Airways and registered as LX-BNG (the last three letters being the initials of Benjamin Nathanial Goldberg, one of the company directors) but was then acquired by BUAF and re-registered G-ASDC. When delivered on 26 March it carried the name 'Pont du Rhin' and completed its first scheduled service flight to Rotterdam that same day.

Seen shortly after arrival at Stansted in August 1962 is X-BNG, a C54A of Interocean Airways, being defuelled prior to removal of engines and outboard wing sections. During the subsequent conversion to Carvair number 7 the airframe was purchased by BUAF for £8,000 (but the deal did not include the engines) and became G-ASDC.

Behind is aircraft number 4, G-ARSH, prior to being temporarily registered as G-41-2, in the final states of completion whilst awaiting fuel flow tests. It became N9758F, the first of two purchased by Intercontinental and then passed on to Interocean Airways for a further UN contract in the Congo.

(ATEL photo via Terry Leighton)

The second of the Aer Lingus Carvairs, conversion No. 8, was completed on 19 April and test-flown that day. Registered EI-AMR and with the name 'Larflaith' (St Jarlath) it was delivered ten days later to Dublin for crew training to commence.

British United Air Ferries' fifth Carvair, the ninth to be built, flew on 8 June and one week later was delivered as G-ASHZ. It had been BUAF's intention to name each aircraft on 'the bridge' after a bridge at or near the operating airport in each country, and 'SHZ went on its first flight on the afternoon of the delivery day to Rotterdam where with due ceremony it was christened 'Maasbrug' by the Burgermistress of that city. A publicity flight around the locality by 'SHZ with BUAF officials and civic dignitaries on board ended the occasion.

In parallel with its Carvair re-equipment programme BUAF also added upgraded terminal facilities to its Southend base. The new building, designed and built by ATEL at a cost of £150,000, was opened in July in order to cope with the increase in traffic which for 1963 alone had been projected to be in the order of 45,000 vehicles, 180,000 passengers and 15,000 tons of freight. Additional vehicle gates and improved passenger handling were the main features.

Carvair No. 10 flew on 29 July registered as G-ASKG and was received by BUAF on 7 August, but the following day it was delivered along with the necessary crews to Alisud (Compagnia Aerea Meridionale of Naples). On 14 August Alisud began a once-daily service from Naples to Palermo, Sicily, with very little advance publicity, and with flight times of just over one hour it was a vast improvement over the nine hour journey by sea. Of six months duration the lease was set up by Dick Worthington, BUAF's sales manager, and the aircraft primarily flown by Don Cartlidge, who had been seconded by BUAF to captain the services for five months before handing over to the BUAF crews to carry on.

G-ASKG seen shortly after delivery to Alisud at Naples with company staff experiencing their first attempts at loading vehicles into the hold. The name 'Channel Bridge' has now been removed from the cockpit sides.   *(Don Cartlidge photo)*

The option was given to Alisud of purchasing the aircraft, as there arose the possibility of expanding what became known as the Tirrenian Air Bridge to link Sardinia with Naples. Alisud had always envisaged raising the number of aircraft on the car ferry routes to three but this did not happen, due partly to them encountering licensing difficulties in 1964 when no services were operated, and partly to them being in direct competition with Interocean who had just pulled their aircraft and services out of the Belgian Congo. On expiry of its lease to Alisud 'SKG returned to BUAF on 25 February 1964 and was put into service with the name 'Channel Bridge'.

1964 – Spain and the deep-penetration routes

Although Aviation Traders had not produced an aircraft for test flying since G-ASKG in July of the previous year production was continuing but interrupted on 8 January 1964 by an incident involving the first Carvair delivered to Aer Lingus. The Irish operator was the main one to come back to Aviation Traders for snags or the like, and always for servicing or checks, and it was for the latter reason that EI-AMP came over. On landing at Stansted after the flight from Dublin the noseleg collapsed but the first indication the crew had was when the aircraft failed to respond to nosewheel steering upon attempting to turn off the active runway. The captain radioed the tower for assistance and requested a tractor tow off the runway as the full extent of the problem was not known. When the recovery tractor arrived it was seen that the noseleg had virtually collapsed but was still providing some support such that the aircraft was able to be towed to the hangar.

Investigations showed that after the aircraft had been towed into position on the flight line at Dublin the toggle pin had not been replaced in the nosewheel torque links, but with the aircraft weight on the undercarriage and the oleo leg compressed the torque links stayed together, thus allowing the pilot to steer out onto the runway. On becoming airborne the undercarriage oleo extended and the torque links fell apart but the fault was not realised until the landing at Stansted when the noseleg spun round with no steering being possible. Being disconnected from the anti-shimmy device the noseleg vibrated badly on touch-down and was finally wrenched sideways, taking the sidewall beam up through the freight floor. If any aircraft with a nosewheel (tricycle) undercarriage was towed with the toggle pin in place and the towing vehicle made a tight turn the whole steering casting could be damaged by the forces on the nosewheel leg being taken directly by the castings of the hydraulic steering mechanism. As it was not possible to employ a flag or other warning device in the system it relied solely on the towing operative remembering to remove or insert the toggle pin at the correct time. After repair, inspection and servicing EI-AMP went back into Aer Lingus service.

Still on the lookout for potential customers, G-ANYB was flown by Don Cartlidge to Fiat at Turin on 20 January for a sales demonstration flight, but due to Turin being fog-bound a weather diversion to Genoa was made. When the weather cleared Turin was reached, and a full cargo of Starfighter parts taken on board, smaller quantities of which had previously been transported by Fiat and Avians Fairey on perilous journeys **through** the Alps to their other facilities at Gosselles and Charleroi by smaller aircraft such as the Bristol Freighter. Although on this occasion the Carvair again demonstrated its ability to shift a considerable amount of freight in one journey it was, however, not employed by Fiat.

The first half of February 1964 was busy with Carvairs No. 13, registered as G-ASKN, flying on the 8th and No. 12, registered initially as G-AOFW, on the 11th. Both had been intended to operate with BUAF but on 18 March 'OFW was leased to Aviacion y Comercio of Madrid, a subsidiary of the Spanish airline Iberia. Trading as Aviaco they operated into and around the Balaeric Islands with domestic freight and passengers but wanted to venture into the vehicle-ferry business.

Shortly after 'OFW emerged as a Carvair Aviaco supplied one of their own C54 types for conversion but, as an interim measure, took that aircraft on lease until theirs was ready. 'OFW was then registered EC-WVD, as was the practice with aeroplanes transferred into Spanish ownership, and delivered to Aviaco on 18 April. It went into service on 1 May as EC-AVD on a once-daily vehicle ferry route from Barcelona to Palma and was operated in the configuration of twenty-two passengers and five cars. With the assured success of this route another, from Valencia to Palma on a three-times weekly basis, was planned.

Although BUAF received 'SKN on 2 March it was not delivered into service until the 26th as 'Pont D'Avignon'. Before ATEL purchased it for conversion it had been left parked at Hamburg for some years, as a result of debts owed, and so much corrosion was found on the wing spars that a stressman had to be sent to Germany to clear it for the ferry flight to Stansted in July 1963. Most of the C54 variants obtained were in a very bad condition and 'SKN was no exception, having been built in February 1943 and the oldest of the type to be converted. Although the C54 had a three-spar fail-safe wing, many reinforcing plates had to be fitted onto 'SKN as part of the conversion before it was deemed airworthy.

On 17 April Carvair No. 14, registered as G-ASKD, had its first flight before being sold to Aer Lingus the following week. Before conversion it too had been static at Hamburg and the subject of a survey before being flown over. Re-registered as EI-ANJ it went into Aer Lingus service as 'Seanen', the Gaelic for St Senan, and made up the initial quota of three. The Irish airline had plans to purchase a fourth vehicle ferry aircraft but this never came to fruition, this last aircraft being operated mainly on the Dublin-United Kingdom routes.

Following the acquisition by BUAF in 1962 of licences to operate Carvairs on the longer 'deep-penetration' vehicle ferry routes to Basle and Strasbourg plans were made to improve the facilities at Lydd Airport. These commenced in 1963 with a new cargo agents block and Customs long room being constructed, and made Lydd one of the most important freight and export/import gateways to the Continent. In March 1964 the main runway, 04/22, was extended by 600' to 5,000' mainly to aid Carvair operations, and new radar and approach lighting aids installed. The secondary runway, 14/32,

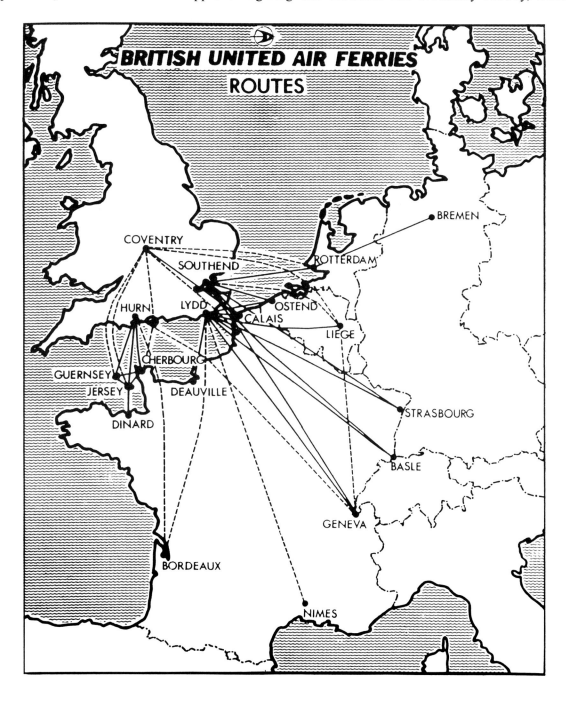

remained unaltered during the life of the airport. These improvements enhanced passenger and vehicle ferry operations, especially on those routes going due south, particularly as Lydd was the primary stepping-off point for the majority of the 'deep-penetration' routes.

The sixteenth Carvair, registered as EC-AEP, left the Stansted production line and was test-flown on 4 June. At the end of the month it was flown back to the owning company, Aviaco, in the ferry markings of EC-WXI as the first of two aircraft (eventually) to be supplied by them for conversion. During the lease of G-AOFW, while conversion of the first Aviaco-owned aircraft was taking place, their vehicle ferry operations had increased to the extent that it was considered building up the fleet to three aircraft by the end of 1964. Along with their own two aircraft EC-AVD, alias G-AOFW, would have been purchased outright from BUAF but a sudden drop in trade meant this did not happen straight away.

Although during the five months up to November 1964 that Aviaco operated the first two aircraft on the car-ferry routes some 3,300 vehicles and various types of freight had been carried, it was realised that the services could be covered by just two aircraft. Aviaco had, coincidentally, sent a second C54 to Stansted for conversion at the beginning of November and had to honour that contract, therefore on 16 November EC-AVD was returned to England where it was put into open store.

1965 – the French and Antipodean connections

Slightly out of order numerically the eleventh Carvair, G-APNH, was test flown on 4 January 1965 and delivered to BUAF on the 10th with the name 'Menai Bridge'. As a C54 it was claimed by Laker as a bad debt and operated out of Southend by Air Charter Ltd during the period that G-ANYB was being converted and test-flown. It was transferred to BUAF at a time when conversion had been halted due to lack of a new owner, and some four months elapsed after the change of ownership before final completion and test flight.

Unlike other production line aircraft so far produced conversion of 'PNH was undertaken at Southend, where the manufacture of ATL98 front fuselages and ancillary components had eased somewhat such that it was considered worthwhile to employ the staff there (many of whom had worked on the mock-up as well as 'NYB) to produce a conversion rather than have them made redundant.

On 8 March 1965 the one-year lease by Aviaco of EC-AVD came to an end and BUAF once again took ownership. The aircraft was re-registered G-AOFW and went back into service on 3 April after repainting and servicing, and was the first of two BUAF Carvairs not to be given a 'bridge' name. Coincidentally, four days after BUAF took back 'OFW the next Carvair to be test-flown was the second aircraft supplied by Aviaco for conversion. With the Spanish registration of EC-WZA it was delivered back to Barcelona at the end of the month, and as Carvair No 18 was the last conversion ordered by Aviaco to make up their fleet of vehicle ferry aircraft in line with current requirements.

Cie Air Transport, a French contemporary of BUAF, bought LX-IOG from Interocean and it became F-BMHV on 31 May with the name of 'Cdt Max Guedjt' This was in honour of a French air ace from the Second World War who had commanded a squadron in the Banff Strike Wing of the Royal Air Force, but was killed in 1945 whilst leading an attack on a German convoy in Norway. A further delivery to CAT on 19 June resulted in LX-IOH, the remaining Interocean Carvair, becoming F-BMHU with the name of 'Henri de Montal', after a famous French entrepeneur.

CAT Carvairs had their fuselage topsides in white with polished aluminium undersides and a normal style blue cheat line carrying the name 'Cie Air Transport'. Beneath the cockpit was the aircraft name with the company emblem below, this being a square motif with aircraft superimposed on a seascape to symbolise the general operational role. The 'Carvair' name was at the fin top, two horizontal black lines at mid-height, and a tricolour at the base.

Expansion by CAT, leading up to the acquisition of two car-ferry aircraft, had been in the form of plans for services in conjunction with Aviaco. These included the possibility of routes from Nimes to Lydd and Palma, and were all in addition to the new Nice-Corsica service started by the company the previous year.

Whilst CAT was still the French agent for Silver City Airways it had previously merged with BAF on the European and cross-channel routes in the years up to 1960, using Bristol Freighters, and with Aviaco on the Palma-Nimes route in June 1965 (both on the basis of pooled services) to produce what was at the time an extremely workable situation. This was however not the case for the other European Carvair operators with bases and/or routes in and around the Mediterranean area.

Within this area the various companies started out by competing directly against each other for the largest possible share of the passenger or mixed freight market and had therefore concentrated their efforts in the direction of the most popular and well-used traffic routes, whereas had they all merged to form one organisation a much greater and more varied sphere of operations could have been encompassed.

While the main emphasis on Carvair usage by Alisud had been the short-haul, domestic 'island-hopping' routes, and by Aviaco its concentration on the main Palma-Barcelona and other internal freight routes, only CAT had gone further with its style of operations. Following the mutual amalgamation with Aviaco CAT had, as a further means of extending its operational lifeline, begun to exploit the long-haul freight role (as had Interocean previously) and was not slow to investigate the possibilities of freight carriage over the African Continent and the middle East, as well as being able to pick up passenger traffic on these routes as the chance arose.

Following the success of Aviation Traders' C54 conversions Air France then made tentative plans to modify similar aircraft to Carvair standard if customers were forthcoming from their associate companies in the North African area, as well as utilising part of their own fleet of some twenty-four aircraft. If work went ahead complete noses would have been supplied by ATEL and the conversions produced at the company's Toulouse base using aircraft from the Air France fleet plus others from associate companies, depending on the interest generated from these and other operators. The project was well advanced in the planning stage, but came to an abrupt halt when a lack of orders for normal production at Toulouse threatened a shutdown of the plant there and the scheme was dropped.

The Carvair concept had now been accepted by the aviation world and its critics and on 14 September 1965 the first aircraft to be sent to England from the Antipodes was completed and test-flown. Conversion of this, a DC4 from the Australian carrier Ansett-ANA, had taken four months and while work was in hand Ansett had been offered a Carvair on lease, but this was declined due to the Australian Civil Aviation Department being undecided as to whether the Carvair should be flown in that country on an amended type certificate or as a new aircraft. The matter was finally resolved, and all objections to Carvair usage dropped, on condition that the operator accept a reduction of 2,000 lbs in the certified maximum take-off weight, i.e. a reduction in payload.

VH-INJ, the first Australian aircraft, was the 19th conversion completed by ATEL and equipped like all three eventually to return to Ansett with a roller floor system capable of handling the international 88" x 108" freight pallet. The roller and guidance system, known as Rolamat, was designed by ATEL to withstand 3G loading and enabled Ansett to carry seven pallets at a time, and to allow for easier loading the loading door frame was widened at the bottom edges by the addition of cutouts. The normal floor line was retained and the four Rolamat tracks positioned such that vehicles could still be carried. Ansett-ANA took delivery of the re-shaped VH-INJ at Southend on 15 September when the log-books were handed over to Captain John Withecomb of Ansett by ATEL Technical Director Bob Batt, then after a 60-hour ferry flight it arrived back in Australia.

Carvairs in Ansett service had the 'standard' scheme for overseas operators, white fuselage topsides and polished aluminium undersides, with a cheat line in green. This line was multi-striped at the nose

Shortly after conversion VH-INJ of Ansett-ANA is seen being trial-loaded with a palletised load from a Hylo Mk 2 at Southend in September 1965. As pure freighters VH-INJ and 'INK also carried 'Air Cargo' below the fuselage cheat line, beneath the company name, and even at this late stage in time the Carvair logo was still specified for the nose and vertical tail surfaces. (ATEL photo)

reducing to a single line aft of the cockpit. The cheat line was repeated on both sides of the engine cowling front portions at approximately one quarter width but, unlike other operators, the 'last two' were not carried on the nosewheel doors.

On 16 October G-APNH was leased from BUAF to Straits Air Freight Express for a New Zealand tour to promote sales of conversions, and to establish if the Carvair would be a viable 'next aircraft' for the company on retirement of their existing Bristol Freighters. It was flown out to New Zealand in the hands of a BUAF crew captained by the company's chief pilot Dudley Scorge and carried a full load of computers for delivery to another customer, but the main aim of the lease was to interest SAFE and other companies into buying the type as a progression from the many Bristols still in use out there.

No offers of sales were forthcoming and as the Carvair was considered by SAFE to be too large an aircraft for use on the domestic services they operated into small regional airfields 'PNH was returned to BUAF after two months in the sun 'down under'.

SAFE meanwhile continued with the use of the Freighter and Wayfarer conversions and for many years were the main operator of these types in quantity on regular services in the world.

Carvair No. 20, registration VH-INK, was the second Ansett-ANA aircraft to be sent over for conversion at Stansted. It was completed on 27 October 1965, test flown and delivered back into service on 4 November. This and VH-INJ were the only DC4 types converted, and the only aircraft on the Carvair list originally delivered as DC4 from the manufacturers after cessation of the Second World War.

Cockpit of production aircraft (G-ARSF shown). Aft of the throttle levers on the centre console can be seen the Decca navigation log, fitted as standard to all 'bridge' aircraft.

(ATEL photo via A.C. Leftley)

1966 – oil, yachts, dolphins and a gold Rolls-Royce

The only Carvair to be delivered in 1966 was G-ATRV which, although listed as No. 15 and delivered to Stansted on 8 November 1963, was slow in the conversion stage due to various reasons within ATEL such that by the time it flew the subsequent Aviaco aircraft and the first two Ansett types had been in service for some time. G-ATRV was test-flown on 23 March and delivered into BUAF service on 1 April. On this first day its inaugural flights, all with the same crew, were from Southend to Rotterdam, then to Manchester and back to Rotterdam once more before it returned to Southend with a new crew later the same day. Throughout its life with the company it remained without a 'bridge' name, only the second of their Carvairs not be given one.

With versatility and simplicity of operation being the Carvair's main attributes it was not long before other concerns with pressing commitments to ship freight by air came to have need of its usefulness. On 3 January 1966, with the embargo put on oil shipments by the United Nations into Zambia less than one month old, civilian operators took over after the use of military air forces had been vetoed. The value of this airlift can be gauged by the fact that in the month prior to the embargo coming into force RAF

Transport Command alone had flown in 178,000 gallons of fuel. One civilian operator employed was Air Ferry Ltd, normally based at Manston, Kent, who leased two BUAF Carvairs to fly the Dar-es-Salaam to Lusaka route as part of the seven-strong civilian charter fleet which replaced the RAF's Brittanias. Without going deeply into the political side of the affair, suffice it to say that for this kind of operation the organised back-up as available from the military was essential, therefore, although Dar-es-Salaam was a RAF air terminal, the hundred or so servicemen on the airlift and stationed there wore civilian clothes for the duration.

As well as oil the Carvairs, G-APNH and 'SKG, transported oil drilling rig spare parts and personnel for their period of stay in Africa and during the entire lease retained the colours of BUAF but the company name on the cockpit sides was overpainted with 'Air Ferry'. It had been anticipated that on return to the United Kingdom the two aircraft (while still on lease to Air Ferry Ltd) would operate from Manston on cross-channel work using crews from BUAF positioned there daily. After the Carvair had proved itself on the vehicle air ferry Air Ferry then made applications in 1964 to the ATLB for licences to operate similar services from Manston to Calais, Le Touquet and Ostende, but these were refused on the basis that the existing sea ferries were already claiming back a fair proportion of the air ferries' newly-acquired custom, both in terms of passengers and freight.

Applications for further services from Manston to Toulouse and Dijon were also rejected as BUAF already had coverage on these routes, but it is worth noting that before becoming a subsidiary of BUAF in 1963 Air Ferry Ltd had operated the Bristol Freighter from Lydd using crews supplied by (then) Silver City Airways.

Among the more unusual loads carried, either by virtue of their size or type, that have been swallowed up easily in the freight holds of the BUAF Carvairs have included industrial vehicles weighing up to 16,000 lbs, ocean-going yachts of up to 6' 0" beam (of which two or three could be carried at any one time) and the supposed gold Rolls-Royce belonging to Auric Goldfinger loaded into G-ASDC at Southend when the aircraft was on a short loan to United Artists for filming part of the James Bond spy film 'Goldfinger' in 1963.

A model of the proposed 'SuperCarvair', with four Rolls-Royce Dart powerplants and the extended upper passenger deck and fin strake, on the ramp at Southend in June 1966 with Carvair G-ATRV and an unidentified Bristol Freighter behind, all in British United livery. (ATEL photo via Terry Leighton)

G-ASDC at Lydd in July 1966 unloading a motor boat using a Freightmaster lift. While not widely used for vehicle-ferry work, this type of lift found its uses in certain applications of bulk freight handling.   *(Ken Bailey photo)*

When the Bristol-SMECMA Olympus 593 turbojet power unit for the first Anglo-French Concorde was shipped to the French works at Toulouse a Carvair from Southend was sent to British Aircraft Corporation at Filton for this very important airlift. Subsequent aircraft of the 'Guppy' type conversion have been used for this work, but in the initial stages of the Concorde project the Carvair was the only aircraft capable of taking such a load.

Other out-of-the-ordinary loads carried have been live dolphins flown to Rotterdam on scheduled flights and a three-ton whale in transit from RAF Binbrook to an oceanarium in Nice. Both these freight items had to be continually sprayed with salt water to stop them 'drying out' on the flights. Again on the sailing scene, BAF Carvairs had at odd intervals carried spare yacht masts, the longest having been in the order of 54' 0" and six or more at a time presented no space problems. The only difficulty found during loading such items was that the masts sagged and a single Hylo alone could not be used, the solution being to employ as much muscle-power as could be found around the ramp!

Apart from the initial objective – to meet a need in the vehicle ferry field – a distinct contribution was made to the freight business in general. The capacious hold of the Carvair was found economical for commodities as low as 7 lbs/cu ft density, such as eight to ten racehorses in boxes, plus their grooms and other attendants, which could be easily carried.

59

1967 – more ups, downs and changes

Although the freight side of their operations was progressing smoothly British United Air Ferries found it necessary to announce on 23 January 1967 that due to a fall-off in traffic on the seven long-haul routes these services would be dropped and the aircraft re-allocated on other tasks as soon as possible. The outcome of the closure of the long-haul routes was that not all of BUAF's Carvair fleet was able to be used economically on the eleven cross-channel routes remaining, as a result of which G-AOFW was flown to Lydd on 7 February and put into open storage. A month later on 5 March G-ANYB, the first ATL98 conversion, was also flown to Lydd on what was to be its last flight, for not only was it surplus to BUAF's current requirements but had also reached the end of its useful life and therefore permanently withdrawn from use.

Various BUAF Carvairs and other types were put in store or parked for odd periods at Lydd, instead of Southend or any of the Continental cross-channel airports, for while the company was the major user there with its operational lease encompassing the greater part of the airport facilities fees relating to non-operations of this type were minimal. Silver City Airways Ltd, as the holding company, still maintained their overall hold on the airport site and re-leased available areas to other concerns whenever possible.

The second accident to a Carvair in service resulting in a write-off occurred on 8 March to F-BMHU, operating with Cie Air Transport (CAT) out of Karachi Airport in Pakistan. Engine failures on the Twin Wasps were quite frequent and a power loss during take-off in this instance caused the aircraft to crash onto the National Highway just after leaving the airport. Both power units on one side failed due possibly to engine mishandling and, with a high humidity atmosphere adding to the reduced performance given by the full freight load being carried, the aircraft lost height rapidly and crashed into the Drigh Road bridge killing four of the crew of six plus seven on the ground travelling in lorries and a rickshaw.

It was somewhat ironic that only a few days earlier Don Cartlidge, previously the senior test pilot for the Carvair programme, had ferried a replacement power unit out to Karachi from Stansted in a Bristol Freighter. This engine was installed in 'MHU and at the time of the accident Cartlidge was still in Karachi. The crew of F-BMHU were returned to Paris for burial, whilst the aircraft was removed from the French register on 19 December 1968.

As a replacement under the sales agreement CAT purchased G-ATRV from BUAF, and on 7 May it became F BOSU on the French register with the name 'President Gamel'. Pierre Gamel had studied pharmacy in Montpelier and set up a practice in Nimes where he became President of the Chamber of Commerce. During the Second World War he was an active member of the French resistance, captured by the Germans he was sent to Buchenwald but survived the ordeal. After the war he returned to business, and later politics before serving two more terms as President of the Chamber of Commerce, he then retired and was made a Commander of the Légion of Honour. He died on 29 March 1966, and just over a year later was honoured by his name being put onto the aircraft.

British United Air Ferries was at this time operating six Carvairs and had two in store at Lydd, those in service carrying the revised BUAF colour scheme comprising a two-tone fuselage cheat line in sand and light blue with a stylised 'bird' emblem on it under the cockpit. The fleet liveries changed again on or about 30 September 1967 when BUAF was purchased out of the Air Holdings group by Mike Keegan and became British Air Ferries. Well known for his earlier exploits in the aircraft sales field when operating from Luton Airport Keegan, together with his sons, revitalised and carried on from Southend the long-established cross-channel services as well as increasing pure-freight carriage to a 24-hour operational basis. At this time BAF was operating the world's only scheduled vehicle-ferry airline, albeit car-carrying figures had dropped since the advent of the hovercraft, but the Carvair concept was still a going concern.

Repainting of the Carvair aircraft was a necessity in order to advertise and present the new company image, but following the usual trends with the type no great changes were made in decor. The fuselage cheat line changed to a two-tone blue and at first the undersides remained in natural metal as before but at some later date the scheme changed to a light blue cheat line and matt dark blue undersides. The use of dark blue undersides arose from a discussion between two of the company directors whereby one, who was smoking the 'Cambridge' brand of cigarettes, produced his own packet and suggested using the same colour as the packet. This was agreed on and the appropriate paint colour obtained.

Shortly after these changes in ownership the second production aircraft, G-ARSD, had its last flight on 4 October and like 'NYB was permanently taken out of service and put into store at Lydd.

Carvairs were still spreading their wings all over the globe, and in some cases shedding them, or parts thereof. On 21 November 1967 F-BOSU, operated by CAT, was over the Sahara Desert on a North African run when the No. 4 engine seized, with the propellor, reduction gear and cowlings breaking away and striking the wing surface. A safe emergency landing was made at Amenas, a desert airstrip, where airframe damage was found to be restricted to the starboard wing and flap. After temporary repairs the aircraft was flown on three engines back to Nimes for full repairs to be carried out.

1968 – Carvairs to Canada

A similar problem befell EI-AMP of Aer Lingus on 2 May 1968 when on an air test from Dublin. During a performance climb with No. 1 engine feathered, this being the critical engine-out configuration, and on passing 7,000 feet the on-board engineer noticed that the oil quantity of No. 3 engine was slowly dropping. He went aft to view the engines and saw fire coming from the outboard side of No. 3 engine. By this time the crew had received a fire warning, the pilot carried out feathering and fire drill and all indications were that the fire had been extinguished and engine revolutions for No. 3 zero, but while re-starting No. 1 engine the pilot noticed that the feathering light for the failed engine was still on. The feathering button was then pulled and the No. 3 engine promptly went into an over-speed condition exceeding 3,000 rpm.

After pulling up the nose of the aircraft to reduce speed the crew were disturbed to see No. 3 propellor shear its shaft and leave the aircraft, striking No. 4 engine on the way and causing some damage to its blades. No. 1 engine was then started without difficulty and the aircraft was able to return to Dublin where it landed safely, although fire was still present in the No. 3 engine and had to be extinguished by the airport fire services.

Subsequent investigations showed that the cause of the fire, and the runaway propellor, arose from the disconnection of the feathering line where it passed through the bulkhead separating the power section from the auxiliary section. (Of the four occasions involving a single engine failure three related to the No 3 position – coincidence?)

EI-AMP was repaired for the second time whilst in Aer Lingus service and, within two months of the incident sold, along with 'AMR and 'ANJ, to Eastern Provincial Airways (1963) Ltd of Gander, Newfoundland. The need for disposal of the aircraft had first arisen in 1966 when vehicle ferry operations had dropped by about 12%, the result being that the service from Dublin to Liverpool was withdrawn and the routes from Dublin to Bristol and Cherbourg, and Cork to Bristol carefully analysed. The decline in traffic continued until 1968 when further use of the Carvair fleet was deemed uneconomical and it was decided to dispose of all three aircraft.

On change of ownership the colour scheme altered, the fuselage cheat line from Aer Lingus Winchester Green to EPA's flame red, with other exterior changes being the substitution of EPA titling and their stylised 'flying goose' emblem on the fin and rudder. Internally very few changes were made, the seating being revised from the standard 22-seat rear cabin to a maximum passenger capacity of 70 and the heating system doubled in order to cope with the colder extremes of the Canadian climate.

The increase in size of the heating system made it necessary to move the heater unit to a location at the rear of the flight deck, which altered the position of the exhaust that had previously been piped out

On the Southend ramp EI-AMP. with 'St Albert' removed from below the cockpit, awaits its turn to be resprayed in EPA colours as CF-EPX, whilst EI-AMR in the background has already become CF-EPV. Out of camera EI-ANJ is in the hangar being worked on before becoming CF-EPW.

(ATEL photo via Dick Worthington)

under the port cockpit window such that it now came out on the down-sloping part of the fuselage hump. It also became necessary to have two intakes to cope with the system's greater requirement for air, these being positioned one either side of the cockpit at the rear of the flight deck.

One other change made to the Carvair for EPA service was the addition of a hatch on the underside of the nose, to be used for mail drops to small settlements where a landing was not possible, or the route time did not allow one. Installed between the nose door cill and the front of the nosegear door the hatch was used by the second pilot in the old-fashioned bomb aimer style.

All the aircraft had returned to Southend for servicing and repainting before the change of ownership and were ferried out to Gander from there. EPA took delivery of their Carvairs on a one-a-month basis, which gave enough time for crew training before the next arrived and was put into service. The first to go was EI-AMR as CF-EPV on 24 May, followed by EI-ANJ as CF-EPW on 6 June and EI-AMP as CF-EPX on 5 July 1968.

On 12 July Carvair No. 21, supposedly the last on the production list, flew on air test. As another Ansett-ANA machine, it had retained its Australian registration of VH-INM during conversion and was ferried back to Australia the following week. Although just under three years had elapsed since the previous conversions had been completed for the company the carriage of freight was still at a level to warrant the use of another such aircraft, so the fleet had been examined earlier for a suitable example. Unlike its predecessors from Ansett VH-INM was a C54E, and with G-ATRV (Carvair No. 15) were the only examples of this particular sub-type completed to Carvair standard. Built to exactly the same specification as the previous two Carvairs for Ansett the inclusion of 'INM for conversion had come at a time when the production line at Stansted was being run down therefore, after Customs clearance, the aircraft stayed at Southend for the modification work. It was ironic that all the work on this, the last conversion, as well as the first and midway No 11, should be carried out at this base.

The summer of 1968 saw a BAF Carvair bring over from Calais a stone signpost weighing over half a ton. This particular signpost, bearing the French town name 'Embry', prompted the escape from his German captors of the then Wing Commander Basil Embry (known as Smith when he flew over enemy territory) when in the vicinity after being shot down in 1940. After spending some time at a new Whitbread public house in London called 'The Escape' it was transferred to the RAF Museum at Hendon where it now forms part of the Escape and Evasion section.

In August Carvair G-ASKN was leased from BAF for a sales campaign of a different kind. With the intention of using the Carvair as a flying exhibition hall a keen London marketing executive, Colin Beale, decided that the 665 square feet of unobstructed floor space ideally suited his purposes. The aim of the venture was to eliminate the time normally taken, and expenses incurred, in setting up, dismantling and moving displays by leasing out part or all of the floor area to an advertiser or corporation who would then have their own material installed and the aircraft flown around to venues likely to attract potential customers. The aircraft would be operated as CB Flying Showcases on hire from BAF, who would provide the operating crews and necessary servicing facilities for the short term leases.

G-ASKN was repainted with CB Flying Showcases, instead of British Air Ferries, on the fuselage and the interior stripped of all seats. The rear passenger cabin was kept intact but converted into a sales office area separated from the main display area (the freight hold in the vehicle ferry configuration) by the existing bulkhead. With a conference table fitted on the starboard side provision was also made for a communications centre, film shows and working demonstrations of equipment. Electrical power for all displays and the additional fluorescent strip lighting was provided by means of a portable 115 volt generator.

G-ASHZ taking mixed freight in palletised loads. Quite a high, but often everyday, reach for a fork-lift but once inside the pallets were not easily moved manually up the sloping floor, unlike the Ansett pure-freighter aircraft which had the Rolomat floor system fitted to deal with such routine loads.

(ATEL photo via Terry Leighton)

Freight handlers-eye view of the Carvair hold, in this case an empty G-ASHZ prior to it taking a full load of palletised mixed freight.

The 'restraining straps' at the rear of the hold are warm air ducts serving this area when it became the front passenger compartment for an aircraft in that configuration.

The square frame, known as the 'cathedral', is the cover to the control cables running from the flight deck down to the underfloor, while between it and the fire extinguisher at front left is the access ladder to the flight deck.

After a short while in service it was found that when Hylos 'squared up' to the opening during loading damage was caused to the front bulkhead, subsequently all aircraft had a timber 'buffer' fitted below the cill.

(ATEL photo via Terry Leighton)

One venture planned was the advertising of Whitbread beers in the United States by first crossing the Atlantic then flying round various airports, dispensing goodwill in the form of free samples, but this never came to fruition owing to the limited amount of 'bar stocks' that could be carried to sustain such a tour. Although the venture was shown to the media at Luton Airport the costs by far outweighed the benefits and 'SKN, far from flying an advertising campaign around Britain and the Continent, was returned to BUAF after a very short period of lease.

On 28 September the ex-Aer Lingus Carvair EI-AMP, now with Eastern Provincial Airways at Gander and registered CF-EPX, completed its disaster hat-trick when it was severely damaged at Twin Falls, Newfoundland. In trying to land on a runway of marginal length, where both the approach and runout ends were bounded by waterways, the pilot attempted to touch down as soon as possible but height was lost on approach and the main wheels struck an embankment about eighty feet from the threshold.

On realising the undercarriage had been damaged the pilot overshot but found that No. 2 engine was not developing full power, so it was feathered. It was then established that the left main undercarriage had broken away from the structure and the hydraulic systems had ruptured and were rapidly emptying, as were the fuel tanks to Nos. 2 and 3 engines, so the pilot circled the strip until emergency services arrived at the runway.

A successful landing was made on the remaining right main and nosewheel but after a short landing roll airspeed fell away and the aircraft settled on the left wing and swung off the runway. After a dramatic end to this non-scheduled flight the thirty-three passengers and five crew members were uninjured, but the aircraft was damaged beyond repair and duly removed from the Canadian Civil Aircraft Register on 31 January 1969.

1969 – changes of name and title

More Carvairs then changed ownership. On 20 February 1969 the Spanish carrier Aviaco sent EC-AXI to the Dominican Republic where, now re-registered HI-168, it was put into service with Compania Dominicana de Aviacion (CDA) flying freight and other commodities around the West Indies as part of an aid scheme. On 3 March BAF sold G-ASKG to CAT and it become F-BRPT on the French register, whilst the second Aviaco aircraft, EC-AZA, went to the Dominican Republic on 22 March to become HI-172.

It will have been noticed that, in the run of aircraft delivered, one construction number has not yet appeared against a rollout or first flight date. Aircraft number seventeen, by now registered as G-AXAI, had first entered the Stansted production line on 10 February 1964 but shortly after being converted to the ATL98 fuselage configuration was still unsold and work stopped. The aircraft, less engines, was put into open store outside Traders' Hangar 4 for over four years and although technically 'cocooned' was used from time to time in supplying parts needed for other aircraft assured of a buyer whilst on the line.

On 19 February 1969 the almost-complete (structurally) aircraft was purchased by BAF at a time when the production line had moved to Southend after conversion of the last Ansett aircraft, therefore ATEL decided to finish the work at Stansted rather than dismantle and ship the aircraft to Southend. However, owing to so many parts having been robbed from the static airframe, it required much remedial work **before** any further conversion could proceed and the ATEL workforce, by now out of practice with Carvair production, were repeatedly stopping work whilst the necessary replacements parts were obtained or made. 'XAI was put into Hangar 4, which had been used for servicing Bristol Britannias of the RAF employed on trooping runs into Cyprus and Singapore at the time ATL98 production was set up. Final completion was on 2 April when it was test-flown and three days later delivered to BAF with the name 'Fat Albert'. Some five years after it first entered the line it became the last production ATL98 Carvair and was also, coincidentally, the last of the C54 types to have come from Interocean Airways S.A.

The employment of the slang names carried by the Carvairs in the BAF fleet at this period in time was a complete change from the meaningful 'bridge' links they had previously worn when being used on the Channel Air Bridge by British United Air Ferries. The origin of the names came about as a result of constant references made by BAF staff to the large bulk and ungainly shape of the aircraft and were eventually picked up at management level, consequently when the aircraft went in one at a time for maintenance checks in this period the various names were applied, G-AXAI becoming 'Fat Albert'.

On 29 April, after being taken out of open storage at Lydd and serviced, G-AOFW was put back into BAF service carrying the name 'Big John'. This brought the number of Carvairs in the fleet back up to six, being the mean operating number that BAF had for the present time the intention of retaining.

One of the main reasons for the success of the cross-channel services from Lydd had been that the distance operated over the main route, to Le Touquet, was only 37 nautical miles. If an aircraft (or even two) went unserviceable on this short route it was possible to catch up on the service with the remaining aircraft, whilst being able to get a relief aircraft out or repair the failed aircraft in no time at all. When a Carvair went out of service at, say, Strasbourg (this being the only type with the company capable of such a stage length) it was a 2½-hour trip and a very costly business to rectify the delay and there was no way of catching up with services on these routes.

In winter delays were also brought about by fog or bad weather, and passengers would often relinquish their outward tickets in favour of a short drive to the boat ferry at Dover or Folkestone. Those going eventually by boat always tended to come back by air and most stated that they would still book for air travel the next year as they preferred it to a boat crossing. Some of the charms of going from Lydd were that it was more of a convenient and private airline to use rather than endure the journey via the crowded scheduled airliner or boat ferry.

The car ferry routes from Lydd and Lympne had always appealed particularly to celebrities from the show business world who frequently used the services to travel to and from their Continental engagements. So many film stars and other personalities passed through Lydd that the airport staff rarely took any notice of them. Politicians and diplomats also used the services and many of these are noted in the visitors book normally only brought out for special occasions. HRH the Prince Philip, who originally opened the airport, heads the list of signatures of such dignatories as King Hussein of Jordan, King Fiesel of Iraq and HRH Prince Charles, the Prince of Wales.

Other famous persons noted as having passed through Lydd, especially during the time the Bristol Freighters were operating, included Edward Heath MP and George Brown MP, who travelled on the same day – but not on the same aircraft. Sir Harold Macmillan also took advantage of the regularity of the services, as did Group Captain Peter Townsend when he, at the end of his associations with a certain Royal princess in 1953, left from Lympne for the post of Air Attache in Brussels.

So much had Lydd been associated with the car ferry that even into the 1970s prospective users were still telephoning for bookings, or even turning up, hoping to get their car and family onto that short hop to Europe.

The Carvair services initiated in the Dominican Republic by CDA using the two ex-Aviaco aircraft had proved very successful but were curtailed rather unexpectedly by a spectacular crash at Miami on 23 June 1969 involving HI-168, the first aircraft received from Aviaco. Scheduled as Cargo Flight 402 HI-168 had taken off, after three abortive attempts, from Miami International Airport bound for Santo Domingo with a three-man crew plus a non-revenue Dominican Republic military pilot and a full load of freight. On passing the end of runway 12 after the eventual takeoff the flight was advised by the control tower that heavy white smoke was being emitted from the No. 2 engine and that they were cleared for a priority landing on any runway.

The captain acknowledged this communication and radioed that they were returning to the airport but subsequent eye-witness reports were somewhat confusing. Large puffs of black smoke had been observed in the vicinity of the No. 4 engine prior to the emission of white smoke from the No. 2 but the aircraft continued to climb on runway heading for a short distance until it attained an altitude of approximately 500 feet. The propellor of the No. 4 engine was feathered shortly after take-off but the white smoke from the No. 2 engine then intensified, a left turn back towards the airport was initiated but as it continued altitude was lost and the aircraft crashed into buildings one mile from the approach to runway 27.

The area of damage caused by the crash extended for about a half-mile, starting with the three-storey building first to be hit, through the tops of several others, a gasoline station and a vehicle body shop before finishing at the intersection of 36th Street and 33rd Avenue. Power lines and telegraph poles were also brought down. The four occupants of the aircraft as well as six persons on the ground were killed, with twelve others being injured. The aircraft, believed to have been loaded to its all-up limit, was destroyed by a combination of the in-flight fire and the conflagration caused by the impact despite efforts of the 14 fire trucks that attended the incident. The Safety Board investigating the accident ruled that the probable cause was the confused actions on the part of the crew while attempting to cope with the catastrophic loss of engine power at a critical stage during takeoff.

1970 – out of use and out of time

HI-168 was finally taken off the Dominican register on 1 January 1970 and on 12 January, six months after the accident, its sister aircraft HI-172 was withdrawn from service and parked at Santo Domingo Airport. It stayed there until 1975 when it had deteriorated to such an extent that it was disposed of for scrap, being purchased by a local hotel, the El Embajador, and placed in their car park. Positioned in a semi-dismantled state with the undercarriage off and the outer wing sections erected vertically at the sides of the fuselage, it was then converted into a discotheque and children's amusement centre. It later became a restaurant and as far as the writer knows it remains there still.

The end of 1969 and the beginning of 1970 saw Carvairs from three operators being taken out of service for various reasons. A noticeable reduction in passenger and freight traffic, compounded by routine or off-peak overhauls, rendered CF-EPV and 'EPW surplus to EPA's requirements and they were taken out of use from October 1969 to September 1970.

Another Carvair withdrawn from use was G-ASDC which, still owned by BAF, crashed on final approach into Rotterdam on 17 February in similar conditions that befell G-ARSF in December 1962. On this occasion a light snowfall resulted in reduced visibility, and as the pilot commenced rounding-out he became dazzled from the glare of full-intensity approach lights against the falling snow and 'Big Louie' struck one line of approach light bars. In the collision the nosewheel was removed and the nose went down onto the runway but enough of the oleo leg remained to act as a skid, which resulted in 'SDC ploughing up the runway before coming to a halt. The three crew and a minimal three passengers were uninjured but damage to both the front fuselage and tips of the propellers to the inboard engines meant 'SDC was out of service for some time while repairs were carried out.

Generally the utilisation of vehicle ferry Carvairs by operators had been found to be very seasonal, as evident from the yearly traffic returns, and it was not surprising that some aircraft were taken out of service for seemingly long periods while others remaining in use with the same company appeared to be overworked, when in fact they were only taking a further small share of the workload. Such was the case with F-BRPT when it was taken off operations by CAT at Le Touquet in the spring of 1970.

F-BRPT was one of the conversions referred to as an ATL98A, the different suffix arising from a modification effected as a means of increasing the aircraft's carrying capacity. This modification applied only to aircraft operating on the cross-channel routes and effectively increased the maximum zero fuel weight (MZFW) by 1,000 lbs simply by installing 250 lbs of lead weights into each wingtip. The weights, in the form of circular plugs, were inserted through access panels on the wing undersurface into snug-fit canisters in the wingtips. The reasoning behind this was that, with the empty aircraft at rest on the ground, the weights reduced the wing dihedral, and in order to return the wings to the normal dihedral when in flight an increase in payload was possible. 500 lbs of freight brought the wings back to the at-rest angle and a similar amount caused a full return to the normal flight angle.

After the modification was installed and the panels sealed up the increases in empty weight, together with the corresponding changes in wing dihedral, were checked at all times so as not to exceed the certified manufacturer's figures. For the majority of Carvair operations, being the short haul cross-channel flights or internal UK routes, the modification brought dividends for it meant that more freight or passengers could be carried to offset slightly the ever-increasing turn-round and operating costs. On the longer routes beyond Northern France and the Low Countries it was not used as the all-up weight increased due to extra fuel carried, the governing factor in all cases being the maximum allowable landing weight plus the fact that all loadings were calculated to be within each 1,000 lb bracket to conform with landing fees which were charged in this manner to MoA rates. On odd occasions when some components were changed or repaired, aircraft that had once been modified to the 'A' standard received unmodified wingtips, but this merely required a reweigh and reversion to the maximum all-up weight as applicable to the standard aircraft.

On 26 August 1970 the first and second production Carvairs, G-ANYB and 'RSD, which had been static at Lydd Airport for some three years were finally reduced to produce prior to British Air Ferries giving up their lease on the site. G-ARSD had a fairly quiet retirement before being broken up by the scrapmen but that of 'NYB was quite eventful. Being parked in open storage for the period of confinement at Lydd both aircraft were naturally exposed to the elements and during the winter months were blown around while picketed, 'NYB at one time being driven into the side of the hangar it was parked near. On another occasion, the 1968 Lydd Air Show, it suffered damage from vandals when it

Seen from the top of the terminal building at Lydd are G-ANYB and G-ARSD, the first two Carvairs, parked to the west of runway 04 prior to being reduced to produce by BAF in late 1970. With engines, wingtips and tail control surfaces removed both aircraft also have the company logos painted out. 'NYB is still wearing the original British United scheme and has a screw jack supporting its tail whilst 'RSD, with its undercarriage collapsed, carries the BAF scheme current at that time. On the left is a wingtip of one of the many Bristol Freighters also scrapped by BAF prior to them leaving Lydd. The electricity pylons in the background follow roughly the line of the railway serving Dungeness power station. *(Ken Bailey photo)*

was broken into whilst parked at the end of the out-of-use runway away from the airshow crowds. Various items including safety equipment were removed by children, and although staff in the control tower saw the unauthorised entries the persons concerned were gone by the time security police arrived. On being broken up both aircraft were disposed of locally for scrap as part of BAF's clearance of the site upon moving its centre of operations to Southend.

Long before BAF's decision to base its operations at Southend it became obvious that new threats to profitable trade had arisen. With roll-on-roll-off sea ferries running scheduled cross-Channel services from Dover and Folkestone in the hands of Townsend Thoresen and others, as well as the hovercraft from Dover and Ramsgate (all in close proximity to Lydd, but even nearer to the Channel 'gap'), traffic was being taken away from the airlines in the coastal areas. With this appreciable drop in traffic BAF's ever-changing policy of personal attention to customers' requirements became focussed on the express handling of freight, whilst retaining the cross-Channel air services in a more streamlined form. Although trade had declined on these routes they could not be given up for, once BAF relinquished their operating licences on the established routes to Rotterdam, Ostende and Le Touquet, another company or concern that succeeded with an application to the ATLB would have ruled out further approaches by the airline for their use. As it was by now uneconomical to keep the Bristol Freighter operating alongside the Carvair it was withdrawn from cross-channel use, the last scheduled flight of the type by BAF from Lydd being on 31 October.

Geographically speaking Lydd had always been at a disadvantage for handling bulk freight, unlike Southend which was served by a main road network with a rail link nearby. Lydd had no direct link with the main routes used by haulage operatives and the absence of the long-promised rail link with Ashford, proposed some years previously but never realising anything more than studied interest, was another major factor which influenced the ultimate departure of BAF from its foremost coast-to-coast stepping-off point.

1971 – goodbye to Lydd

Lydd employees had for some time known that the vehicle ferry era was coming to an end there, as soon as they began to see Carvairs going past and 'over the top' to Continental destinations. On 29 January 1971, just prior to relinquishing its lease of Lydd, BAF flew its last scheduled vehicle ferry operation from the site when a Carvair service went out to Ostende, and on its departure Lydd's long association with the vehicle ferry era, nearly 17 years, came to a close.

Even though BAF was now operating solely from Southend, and many of the Lydd staff had transferred there, the general atmosphere of vehicle air ferry operations had changed completely. Only memories remained of the halcyon cross-Channel days, the busy periods when one aeroplane was being loaded, with another taxi-ing out past an arrival, and one on landing approach, and the ground crews moved everything (including themselves) at a brisk pace. With the Bristol Freighter a 'busy' turnround time was eight minutes and operations increased to 70 services per day, peaking at 100 during the summer, but with mechanised bulk freight handling now becoming the norm more vehicles and less people were involved.

The next Carvair to pass into the hands of the breakers was G-APNH, badly damaged on 18 March 1971 following a scheduled BAF passenger flight into Le Touquet. Very severe crosswind conditions existed at the time and although a procedure approach was made to Runway 14, with the main wheels touching first, as soon as the nosewheel contacted the surface it collapsed and the aircraft skidded along the centreline on its front under-fuselage for some distance before finally coming to a halt 1,600 yds after the threshold.

There was no injury to the crew of seven or the eleven passengers but airframe damage, in the form of severe deformation of the fuselage skinning, as well as that suffered by the undercarriage itself, made it unlikely to be repaired. Accordingly G-APNH was put up for scrapping, the fuselage being disposed of locally and the engines plus other usable parts returning to England. De-registry of 'PNH followed on 2 June 1971.

Aviation Traders had for some time kept spare fuselage front sections in store at Southend ready for shipping to Stansted should the need ever arise to repair a similarly damaged Carvair in this country, but it was realised that the work involved in recovery to Stansted and changing the nose would be too costly. As no further conversions were planned the two remaining noses and their special transporter were put up for scrap on 4 May 1971.

1972 – cutbacks and comfort improvements

In 1972 Compagnie Air Transport (CAT) cut back on the size of its Carvair fleet, as the car ferry traffic in the Mediterranean area had declined to such an extent that further use of all three aircraft would have proved uneconomical. It was therefore decided to scrap one aircraft and keep the remaining two in service for a further year. F-BOSU had been first withdrawn from service at Le Touquet in the summer of 1970, before being finally declared surplus to requirements and transferred to associate company Air Fret on 17 April 1972. It was flown to CAT's main operating base at Nimes-Garons and reduced to produce there by BAF engineers at the end of April 1972. The odd thing is that although F-BOSU was not on the operational returns for December 1973 it was still on insurance until June 1974.

Seen at Nimes after removal of engines, rudder and elevators, and with the nosewheel collapsed (the whole unit was later literally cut out of the fuselage, along with the skinning) F-BOSU, 'President Gamel', awaits the torch in April 1972. Although a rather inopportune moment to be photographed it nevertheless shows the CAT insignia and logos to advantage. (John Simms photo)

The following month, in Canada, another of the EPA Carvairs came to grief when landing at Gander on 3 May. The aircraft, CF-EPV, touched down after a local flight but as soon as the nosewheel contacted the runway and braking commenced the nosegear retracted and caused severe damage to the underside of the nose and propellors of the inboard engines in a similar manner to G-APNH a year previously. With a provisional reserve on this claim of $75,000, repairs to 'EPV were carried out by EPA engineers using DC4 spares obtained in Canada along with parts of one of the stored ATEL front fuselage units which was shipped out via London (Heathrow) Airport. The aircraft returned in service with EPA until sold to Robert C.S. Graham, a shipping agent of Prince Rupert, British Columbia, in October 1973.

By the end of 1972 the Carvairs owned by BAF had been engaged on car ferry work for some ten years, having been used incessantly on the cross-channel routes, and accordingly their condition had deteriorated externally to quite an unkempt appearance. No replacement for the type seemed immediately forthcoming, and although the proposed Brittan-Norman Mainlander had been shown in model form at the previous year's Paris Air Show carrying the colours of BAF this progressed no further than the scheme stage. BAF therefore made moves to improve the comfort and appearance of their fleet for the 1973 summer season.

Passenger accommodation in the rear cabin was reduced from the original figure of twenty-one to seventeen, thus giving more leg space while still retaining the intimate atmosphere, the interiors were completely refurbished and taped music facilities added. Externally the changes were limited to a revision of the colour scheme in that the fuselage cheat line was now light blue only, but still extending up to the fin top, with the fuselage undersides and wing surfaces in dark blue. The upper fuselage remained in white and the presence of the personal slang names became even more noticeable.

1973 – slang names and steering problems

Early in 1973 the number of Carvairs carrying slang names increased when CAT finally decided to dispose of its two remaining aircraft. On 23 February F-BMHV came onto the British register once more as G-AREK, being taken over by BAF and named 'Porky Pete', whilst on 26 March F-BRPT became G-ASKG with the name 'Big Joe'.

Back in Canada the remaining undamaged ex-Eastern Provincial Airways aircraft, CF-EPW, had its own share of the publicity on 20 April when it was damaged during the course of a crew training programme at Gander Airport. Three days earlier it had been purchased by Robert C.S. Graham, who then immediately leased it to Norwegian Overseas Airways, based in Oslo, and at the time of the incident it was being crewed by Norwegian personnel from that company.

After landing to change pilots a 180 degree turn was initiated in order to back-track to the take-off point but after a few degrees of turn nosewheel steering was lost and the aircraft stopped. The flight engineer then left the aircraft to inspect the nosegear and reported that although the nosewheel was now straight and the scissor links in place the oleo unit was almost fully extended, thus isolating the wheel from the steering mechanism. On informing the pilot, who then tried unsuccessfully to 'castor' the nosewheel while steering with engine power, it was decided to apply the brakes in order to bring the nose down and re-engage the steering mechanism but on doing this the nose oleo leg fractured, causing the nose of the aircraft to drop and hit the runway. The crew immediately exited the aircraft over the left wing, using the escape hatches on that side, and prepared to fight any fire but his was not necessary as the pilot had already completed the shut-down checklist.

CF-EPW was damaged in the now-familiar pattern of inboard propellers and underside of nose and duly removed to the maintenance workshops, where it was repaired by the EPA engineers in a similar manner to that of CF-EPV. This type of incident involving loss of directional steering generally arose as a result of loading the aircraft with its c.g. too far aft, thus causing the nose to rise above the normal position for engagement of the steering gear, and Aviation Traders had recommended the use of the tail prop common to C54 and DC4 types in order to gauge if the aircraft was properly loaded. The prop was bolted on through the tail bumper and after loading was complete checked to ensure that it was clear of the ground. Loading the aircraft slightly forward of the c.g. position was not critical.

As far as the story of the Carvair on vehicle-ferry and associated operations is concerned this was the last incident in the eleven years of operation from 1962. Of the eleven reportable incidents six were due to failure of the nosegear, three to crashes (one due to weather and two to engines) and two to in-flight-emergencies resulting from engine failures. Five aircraft were written off due to these, the others being returned to service after repair. Of the aircrews nine members died, two suffered serious injuries and 24 had minor injuries. As to other persons involved, either as passengers or on the ground, 12 were seriously injured and 61 slightly.

Ansett-ANA in Australia had by now already started to phase out the Carvairs it had in service in favour of up-to-date jet transports and the intention was to dispose of as much of its piston-engined fleet as soon as possible, whilst retaining its Lockheed Electras, but had previously been unable (since at least 1968) to arrive at an agreeable decision with its associate company, Trans Australia Airlines, over the choice of freighter aircraft.

Eventually Ansett acquired suitable jet transports and the Carvairs were taken out of use at Sydney and put into open storage pending disposal. VH-INJ was the first to be sold, going to Royal Air Cambodge and appearing on the Cambodian register as N33AC from 3 July.

It was given the name 'Barb' and based at Phnom Penh, where it was in use throughout the 1974/75 hostilities in North Vietnam and Cambodia, before being damaged during a mortar attack on the base whilst movement of the Cambodian forces was taking place. As it was impossible to carry out suitable repairs it was struck off charge and left abandoned on the military side of the airbase as a decoy for any further attacks. The remaining two Ansett aircraft meanwhile were still at Sydney under new ownership, having been taken over by the Australian Aircraft Sales company in January 1974.

N33AC, previously VH-INJ of Ansett, in the colours of Air Cambodge at Phnom Penh in February 1974. A red fuselage cheat line separates the polished metal undersides from the white topsides with the name 'Barb' under the cockpit and the Cambodian flag just forward of the company name. Unusually both halves of the rear entry door are in use for loading, normally the rear half was kept fixed.

On 3 August the lease of CF-EPW to Norwegian Overseas Airways ended. In June it had been ferried from Gander to Southend for servicing and repainting before being sub-leased to BAF on 6 August, it then regained its British registration of G-ASKD and went back into service repainted in BAF's colours.

The following month CF-EPV took the same route and on 3 October was then leased to Norwegian Overseas Airways, but after being ferried to Southend for servicing stayed with NOA and while on lease to them retained its Canadian registration and EPA colours but without that company's insignia.

The work was completed as requested but no settlement was forthcoming, accordingly the aircraft was impounded under a court order and parked on the apron. After a while the engines were removed for use on other aircraft and it seemed that the aircraft would be cannibalised but this was not so and it remained static.

1974 – Pauling takes on 'Porky Pete'

Carvair No 5, G-AREK, which had flown with BAF as 'Porky Pete' ever since its return to the United Kingdom, left the company on 20 June 1974 when it was sold to Pauling Co., a civil engineering concern engaged on extensive construction work in the Middle East. Although ownership and country of operation changed the aircraft still retained its British registration and was therefore still certified to carry passenger traffic when required to do so in addition to the freight it regularly transported between Abu Dhabi and Midway, two regional airports in Saudi Arabia. The Pauling emblem painted on 'REK to replace the BAF insignia was a projected map of the world, centred on the North Pole, thus depicting the company's wide sphere of operations. The characters on the emblem were in English on the port cockpit side and starboard fin and rudder, whilst on the opposite sides they were in Arabic. In addition the broad blue BAF fuselage cheat line was replaced by yellow on both sides but the remainder of the scheme was unchanged.

G-AREK at Southend in July 1974. The dark blue BAF colour remains to the undersides but with a yellow fuselage cheat line sweeping up to the fin and rudder on the white topsides. The Pauling 'globe' insignia in blue and yellow is prominent with its characters in black alternating in English and Arabic at each position.   *(John Simms photo)*

1975 – Norway, no way, no paint

BAF relinquished its lease of G-ASKD on 11 November 1974 and on 2 February 1975 it was delivered to Norway. Purchased by Rorosfly Cargo Norway it was re-registered as LN-NAA and repainted in their colours, this being the basic BAF scheme but with the undersides painted light grey and new insignia added. The name under the cockpit became RFN and the individual name of 'Viking North Sea Express' was complemented by a small winged Viking helmet.

After working the Oslo-Kristiansund route for a short period the aircraft, far from being put to use in working a car ferry/mixed freight role, was transferred to the International Red Cross and repainted

LN-NAA in two guises. The upper photo was taken at Southend in February 1975 with it wearing Rorosfly Cargo Norway colours whilst the lower, taken at Basle later that same year, shows the International Red Cross scheme applied for the proposed aid flights to the Far East, which terminated with the aircraft being impounded at Bangkok. The dark area at the rear of the upper deck is the heater exhaust shield, required when the enlarged system was installed to cope with the extremes of the Canadian climate.
(John Simms photos)

white overall with large red crosses and the new operator's name prominently displayed. It left for the Far East, via Basle, Bahrain and Bangkok, ostensibly to work on famine and disaster relief, but as fees owing to servicing and repair companies were not settled it was impounded at Bangkok and held there by federal authorities until outstanding bills were paid.

At the end of 1974 BAF had realised that the many paint layers resulting from the various company schemes on each of its Carvairs bestowed a weight penalty and decided that, as an exercise, one of the fleet would undergo a lightening operation in order to see if any more load could be usefully carried as cargo. Freight operations had at this time become more of a viable proposition than the car ferry services due to a drop in the number of passengers travelling with their own vehicles, and the idea for a new configuration also coincided with a London docks strike involving baggage and freight handlers.

An aircraft acquires a considerable amount of excess weight whilst in service, either by the repair of exterior skinning due to damage or corrosion, revisions to exterior paintwork or addition of extra equipment on change of use or ownership. As the aircraft empty weight increases the amount of payload carried is reduced, so as not to exceed the all-up weight.

The aircraft chosen by BAF for the experiment was G-ASDC, and on examining the whole structure it was found to be carrying far more paint than could be accepted. Removal of the exterior paint was the first priority and together with all interior fittings, save for five seats for the use of accompanying marshals and loaders, nothing remained which would add unnecessary weight. The initial aim was to enable a further 1½ short tons (3,000 lbs) to be carried, and when the excess surface drag and weight of the paintwork had been eliminated by its removal it was calculated that one ton could be added to the payload. Removing the seats and fittings gave another half ton and when 'SDC, now renamed 'Plain Jane', made its debut on 11 February 1975 it showed off a highly-polished bare metal finish with the new slogans 'BAF Cargo - 8½ tons payload' as its only embellishments.

G-ASDC, in its new role as Cargo Freighter 'Plain Jane', loading racehorses for France at Southend. The special horsebox designed by BAF sits on the Hylo platform whilst another customer waits below. Behind the nosewheel can be seen ATEL director Bob Batt's Percival Prentice G-APJB, a long term resident at the airport.   *(Keith Yuill photo via BAF)*

After conversion G-ASDC contributed greatly to BAF's load-carrying capabilities and in the first weeks after it returned to service it was hardly ever static, such was the demand for the all-freight Carvair version. In the summer of 1975 the viability of the new scheme was demonstrated when, in one journey, 'Plain Jane' uplifted all the instruments for the Vienna State Philharmonic Orchestra to an engagement in the north of Scotland. Other exponents of the live music scene such as bandleaders Geoff Love and Kenny Ball have also used the facility to travel between engagements.

In August 1975 G-AOFW again went on lease, this time to a pop music company and was used for a month carrying artistes and equipment around Europe. In the form of a 'wet' lease, by which BAF provided the crews and any servicing, the only change in the aircraft was the addition of a large futuristic spaceman emblem with the legend 'BTM presents Startrukkin' 75' behind the cockpit windows on both sides, all this being painted out when the lease ended and the aircraft was returned to BAF. The musicians found the Carvair to be ideal for their purposes, and while they were able to relax in the rear cabin or plan the next event all their necessary goods and trappings were stowed away up front. Some of the items carried included cars as well as clarinets but all were well catered for.

The 'Startrukkin' 75' hire was really the last of the outstanding and memorable leases taken on by the Carvair, previous lessees having included The Who, Small Faces, Shirley Bassey and Alvin Stardust. Other memorable passengers have included John Mills, King Hussein of Jordan and Crown Prince Gustav of Sweden. On a lighter vein whole crateloads of rabbits, monkeys, snakes and geese have been carried, but probably not as noisily as the numerous rugby teams who have insisted on revelling with or without trousers on! Other passengers who fall into the 'memorable' category have included coffins with contents, the group of drunken seamen who fell out of the door after the airsteps had gone, and the many people who have opened the passenger door in flight instead of that to the toilet. Ah, those long-forgotten, halcyon days of flying, when will they return?

On receipt of an enquiry from an overseas operator G-ASKG was soon on the move and, with the sale resulting in the aircraft going to SOACO of Libreville, Gabon (previously French West Africa), it meant that Carvairs had now been owned and operated in all of the five Continents. 'Big Joe', as it had been known in BAF service, was re-registered as TR-LUP before it left Southend on 21 February 1975 and carried the name of SOACO on the fuselage instead of British Air Ferries, but otherwise the colour scheme remained the same.

As with most of the single-type operators their aircraft were sent away for repairs or the periodic maintenance to a separate facility. In the case of SOACO these were undertaken by Air Africa at Brazzaville and in March 1976 when TR-LUP was due for a Check 4 it was completely overhauled and repainted. The new scheme chosen by SOACO was very similar to that of Aer Lingus, being a white upper fuselage with aluminium undersides and a green fuselage cheat line, the entrance door and emergency exits also being lined in green. The company name appeared on the fuselage sides and, as a reminder of its earlier European operations, the name 'Big Joe' was retained on both sides under the cockpit windows.

SOACO, standing for Société Anonyme de Constructions, operated TR-LUP in very much the same way as did Pauling Ltd with G-AREK in the Middle East, namely for transporting construction tools, materials and labour in and around the Gabonese Republic from its main base at Libreville. The majority of flights were in the order of one or two hours and the aircraft, amassing about 100 hours per month, was normally operated by a crew of two.

By late 1975, when vehicles accounted for less than 5% of total traffic on all of its routes, British Air Ferries began to concentrate more on the use of its Carvairs for the carriage of freight and immediate charter work. However, in the summer of 1975, a seasonal increase in Continental air traffic made BAF aware of the need to reintroduce a service to Basle in Switzerland, this being one of the deep-penetration car ferry routes originally dropped by BUAF in 1967 when passenger figures had begun to decline. The unexpected demand was such that a three-times-weekly service was reopened, using the Carvair in the now-usual 17-seat configuration with space for freight or cars as before in the main cargo hold.

In February, March and July of 1975 BAF had acquired three Handley Page Heralds from Eastern Provincial Airways for use on the Continental passenger routes. This aircraft could seat up to 50 passengers in a pressurised cabin and the greater speed offered by the type reduced flight times on the cross-channel routes by a quarter of those previously recorded by the Carvairs. Prior to this BAF had on occasions leased other suitable passenger aircraft such as the Hawker Siddeley 748, but the Heralds were the first all-passenger types to be purchased outright by the airline since the emergence of BUAF in 1962.

The first two Heralds in service carried BAF colour schemes with the individual names of 'Rupert Keegan' and 'Jeremy Keegan' (the names of the managing director's sons) but the third underwent a conversion in October for a slightly different role. With luxury seating for 21 passengers in a spacious cabin, and the BAF insignia discreetly absent from the otherwise standard colour scheme, it appeared as an executive aircraft for immediate hire. With slightly cheaper rates than pure jet aircraft of the same status and nearly three times the seating capacity of these types BAF was once again demonstrating its ability to adapt its services to cater for the ever-changing needs of the air transport market.

Although providing a greater level of comfort and increased passenger potential than the Carvair, use of the Herald meant a significant change for cabin staff. The sense of cosiness that had arisen from the original cross-Channel vehicle ferry operations on first the Bristol Freighter and later the Carvair was now lost with the Herald, the larger and more spacious passenger cabin dispelling the familiar intimate atmosphere that had arisen with the compact rear cabin of the previous types. While BAF's operations in car ferry had declined the days of the Carvair with the company were not yet coming to an end, even though the carriage of freight became the main role for the type on the routes still open. Passenger operations however, whilst still maintaining a viable operating level, did not warrant them retaining six aircraft and they were advertised singly for disposal.

1976 – two to Africa and a 'first' at the last

Towards the end of 1975 a French operator in the all-freight business, Secmafer S.A. of Nice, was so impressed by BAF's usage of G-ASDC as an all-cargo Carvair that it decided to purchase G-AXAI from BAF with the intention of using it in the same way. To this end 'XAI was stripped of its finery and colours plus all 55 seats in the front passenger cabin and flown out of Southend for delivery to its new owner. Registered as F-BBEF and in the plain metal finish it was ferried to Nice on 7 January 1976 where the toilet and rear cabin seating layout were to be revised to suit the new operational requirements of Secmafer. On arriving in France however it was not put into immediate use due to the reluctance on the part of the authorities to certify it in its new role, accordingly it was put back onto the British register as G-AXAI until 27 January when type certification had been clarified and the necessary dispensations obtained.

The next 'international' Carvair movement at Southend was the re-appearance of G-AREK, fresh from its use by Pauling Ltd in the dusty Middle East. Overdue for a routine check, its anticipated arrival was delayed due to a temporary diversion to Athens Airport after an in-flight engine failure was experienced on the ferry flight from Saudi Arabia to the United Kingdom. On 11 January BAF, who were to do the servicing, sent a team of engineers out to Athens and made sufficient repairs to enable 'REK to continue on to Southend. Eventual arrival was on 8 February when it was parked on the apron next to CF-EPV, but soon after was moved over to the BAF engineering base on the north side of the airport where three of the propellers were removed for use elsewhere. With one engine left complete it remained parked outside until Pauling Ltd gave full clearance for work to commence.

In the meantime, transport operations by SOACO in Gabon had, in the time elapsed since the purchase of a BAF Carvair, increased such that the need arose for more aircraft of this type. Further approaches to BAF by the company resulted in them acquiring G-ASKN, the aircraft leaving Southend on 10 June en route to Gabon. On arrival the aircraft gained the registration of TR-LWP and was repainted in its new colours in due course.

The upper photo shows G-AXAI, 'Fat Albert', carrying the ultimate BAF vehicle-ferry scheme of white topside, light blue stripe, with dark blue wings and undersides at Southend in November 1975.

The lower photo was taken in January 1976, again at Southend, and shows it after transfer to Secmafer S.A. As an all-cargo freighter only the Tricolour and registration are carried, but here F-BBEF has been temporarily over-painted G-AXAI.   (John Simms photos)

Had SOACO known it, should they have wished to increase their fleet even further without approaching BAF, they could have acted on an advertisment placed in the British aviation press in October of that year. Having taking ownership of the remaining two ex-Ansett Carvairs a New Zealand concern, Dwen Airmotive of Auckland, was offering them for sale as freighters with zero-timed engines plus a large range of support spares.

Now after disposal of roughly half of their Carvair fleet British Air Ferries, the longest-running operator of the type, had changed their mode of operation once again and begun to concentrate on the Dart Heralds for carriage of passengers on the European routes with the freight/vehicle ferry taking very much a back seat. Freight operations using the all-cargo aircraft 'Plain Jane' were still viable but the main activity was centred on the rapid replacement of the company fleet with increasing numbers of Dart Heralds, such that by mid-1977 the number on strength with the company had increased to six.

Shortly before its association with the vehicle air ferry came to an end BAF gained a 'first' when their first female captain on the cross-Channel routes was featured in the local press. By July 1976 26 year-old Caroline Frost had amassed much air time as a first officer on Carvairs and was given command of an all-female crew, but whilst this announcement took petticoat power to new heights (to quote the *Southend Evening Echo* article) the run-down by BAF of its vehicle air ferry services continued.

1977 – the end of an era

After a periodic overhaul in June 1977 Carvair G-ASHZ, 'Fat Annie', was stripped of its paint and converted into the pure freight configuration as had been the case with 'SDC two years previously. By this time the much larger company fleet of Dart Heralds had taken over completely the cross-channel services, making operation of the Carvair in the vehicle air ferry role an unprofitable proposition, and accordingly the remaining company aircraft G-AOFW, 'Big John', was de-engined and put in open storage outside the BAF engineering base on the north side at Southend. During a gale the front loading door was torn off but replaced by that from CF-EPV, broken up in 1978, and it was hoped 'OFW would remain as a memorial to the type but this did not happen and in 1983, despite local appeals and an article in the aviation press, the aircraft was scrapped.

British Air Ferries' G-ASDC, parked in the sun at Sharjah, UAE, on completion of a long-range freight flight in 1976. The bare metal finish on 'Plain Jane' is shown to advantage. (*John Simms photo*)

As the BAF Heralds were wearing new style colours it was decided to have the freighter Carvairs carry them also. These were applied over the bare metal finish on the tail and nose, the latter tending to emphasise even more the hump effect of the front fuselage which had been the main identifying feature of the aircraft for so long.

Although the capability for transporting vehicles and accompanying passengers was still theoretically possible within the operating capabilities of BAF, by the simple expedient of fitting seating units to the Carvairs, the move to pure freight work for the remaining types in the company's fleet dealt the final blow to the vehicle ferry era. After a period of ten years in service with BAF and five with its predecessor British United Air Ferries the Carvair, having taken over the work associated with the vehicle air ferry from the ageing Bristol Freighters, had proved to be a rugged, snag-free design that excelled itself in all the situations unforeseen by the people responsible for its inception.

Conclusions

As with the earlier Bristol Freighter the Carvair was envisaged and used on the European 'commuter' routes, and like its predecessor operated on a world-wide scale in the carriage of vehicles and freight. Had the proposed conversions been carried out to the DC6 and DC7 aircraft, or the turbo-prop Carvair pursued, it is just possible that the design as originally conceived (some years before other aircraft of similar size and configuration) might have been advanced sufficiently enough and at the right time to establish the operators in the forefront of the medium-haul air transport business. As it was some of the shortcomings in the use of the ATL98 which may have led to its decline in use included the unreliability of the powerplants, albeit that these were retained for reasons of availability, and the fact that supplies of 100 octane fuel were now becoming more difficult to obtain en route or at staging points for aircraft on charter.

Had it been decided that the Carvair concept progress to the prop-jet and pure jet era the logical continuation would have been achieved by the production of a Douglas DC6 or DC7 conversion, or a pure-jet freighter as typified at the other end of the size scale by the Lockheed C5A Galaxy. The proposed Dart Carvair, tested in the wind tunnel at the same time as the basic Carvair design, realised no more than interest and was not proceeded with at all. It must be noted that both the DC6 and DC7 were, at the time the ATL98 was being produced, still in regular airline service and would have been extremely expensive to obtain and convert had design approval been given.

The aviation business is built on ever-changing trends; the innovative way of using large helicopters to lift freight panniers has been used now for some time, short take-off and landing aircraft have been in vogue in a number of uses throughout the world, and now large-bodied transports with a certain degree of STOL performance are being pressed into service on all fronts.

The Carvair was a new trend introduced at a time when the British aircraft industry was struggling to keep its head above the waters of technology. Its very existence arose as a result of lengthy discussions between one operator and the aircraft construction companies in general producing no immediate successor to the types in use, whereas another operator in direct opposition not only conceived the right design but implemented its production and subsequently used it successfully in service.

In practical terms

The rear cabin, originally designed to seat 23 but later revised to 17 passengers, gave a sense of intimacy and personal service far removed from the large high-density airliners of the day (and today!). The cabin attendant seated just in view on the passageway seat, and able to be summoned for any reason, retained the personal aspect of the services. Without even having to move from a standing position at the 'galley' any number of tasks could be performed, as all passenger service items were located conveniently within arms reach in this compact area.

The less said about the toilet compartment the better – except to say that its confined but well-equipped space was suitable for the job!

For those travelling in the main cabin when the aircraft was reconfigured to the all-seater layout of, say, 55 passengers the feeling was of a normal airliner due to the absence of any vehicles giving, by comparison, acres of space. One slightly unnerving aspect for the passengers however concerned those occupying the extreme front row of seats. In front of them was the movable bulkhead that separated the cabin from the space left for baggage at the extreme front of the freight deck beneath the cockpit. Whilst the bulkhead was fixed in position for any particular layout it did tend to move with aircraft vibrations such that its connecting door into the baggage area would often spring open and swing to and fro, upon which a sweetly-smiling attendant would appear and attempt to keep it closed . . .

Normal access to the flight deck was by ladder from the freight hold and easy enough with the aircraft on the ground, but in flight the experience of climbing a vertical ladder whilst it is in motion can only be likened to ascending the rigging on a boat. Once through the floor hatch and onto the flight deck the most striking aspect is the noise, for unlike the passenger cabin the flight deck is uninsulated against outside sound, the level being quite deafening until a headset is put on. The Carvair has to be flown with a 'hat' on for even though the propellers are some 20' 0" behind you the engine noise level is incredibly high.

The second thing realised is the sheer amount of space behind the crew seats, due to the humped top decking line. It can be seen why the Interocean aircraft had rest bunks* fitted there for the extra crew members to use on long over-water trips, there is so much space available. (*If you ignore the noise they can be called that).

Sitting behind the pilots in the flight engineer's, or third seat, the cockpit layout can be easily seen. The extra width over the C54 is not that apparent nor is there much difference in the instrument layout, it being a straight 'pinch' from that type.

The most noticeable aspect as far as the flight deck is concerned is the view out of the front windscreen during the landing approach, for when established on finals you are aware just how much higher the crew are than in, say, the C54. On an approach to Runway 24 at Southend (with a landing distance available of 4,770 feet) it appears at first sight that you may not get in, but once the reduced power setting takes the speed down to the 93 knots required a normal approach over the railway line will result in a touchdown just past the numbers. Again, due to the high cockpit level, although you can feel the wheels contact the surface you cannot hear them, but once down steering and braking is normal.

What remains now of the Carvair?

Today only a handful of Carvairs exist in service around the world, albeit that they are operated in a completely different role to that of the vehicle air ferry originally proposed, but of the others very little remains apart from photographs and memories.

The original wind tunnel model, with the proposed turboprop engines and test sections for the extended upper deck added, was on display at the Historic Aircraft Museum, Southend, but with the demise of that organisation its current whereabouts is not known. All that is known to exist from the first production aircraft G-ANYB (scrapped at Lydd in 1970) is the manufacturer's plate, now held by the assistant programme test pilot Bob Langley.

Of the last aircraft in the United Kingdom, a few fragments from G-AOFW (scrapped at Southend in 1983) including cockpit sidescreen glazing and an under-fuselage baggage door are in the author's collection (in 1975 this was the last Carvair the author flew on). The cockpit and flight deck from CF-EPV (scrapped at Southend in 1978) was once on loan to the 100th Bomb Group Museum at Thorpe Abbotts in Norfolk but has now returned to its Halesworth, Suffolk owner, whilst parts of the nose undercarriage from this aircraft are on display in the Thameside Aviation Museum at Tilbury, Essex.

Although the author has only a few fragments a local devotee has, by comparison, gained quite a collection. Jack 'Laurie' Rowe, now retired after many years as captain on Carvairs with BAF, was the instigator of the campaign to save G-AOFW from scrapping but having been beaten by the scrapman had to console himself with one propellor and a few cylinder heads. These grace his garden, where aircraft wheels also serve as garden furniture, and in due course Jack also acquired the unique flying model of Carvair G-ASHZ, made in 1962 by the Leigh model shop Wings and Wheels, which now hangs in his dining room.

Other bits will still turn up. . .

Carvair

The author's children with, on the right, ex-BAF captain Laurie Rowe in his garden and one of the few propellers salvaged from G-AOFW which now graces a garden bed

Appendix 1

ATL98 Specification

Aircraft dimensions

wing span	117' 6"
length o/a	102' 7"
height o/a	29' 10"
wing area	1,462 sq ft
wing dihedral	7°
sweepback	0° (at 40% chord)

Freight hold dimensions

freight hold length	68' 0"
rear cabin length	13' 2"
maximum width	9' 8"
maximum height	6' 9"
usable floor area	665 sq ft
usable volume	4,350 cu ft.

Passenger accommodation:

when configured to carry 5 vehicles: 22 in rear cabin (this was later reduced to 17),

when configured to carry 4 vehicles: 22 in rear cabin and 12 in new cabin to rear portion of freight hold (34 total when operated by Aer Lingus)

when operated by EPA in an all-passenger configuration: 22 in rear and 48 in front cabins (70 total)

with a high-density, close-pitch seating layout in the front cabin a maximum of 85 passengers could be carried, but this layout was not employed by any carrier

All the above layouts used the standard toilet and passenger service items compartments, as well as the normal entry and emergency exit routes. An underfloor baggage hold installed on the starboard side, with access externally from the outside, had a capacity of 151 cu ft.

Weights: Operational (empty) – 41,365 lbs   Total fuel   – 14,800 lbs
Maximum payload   – 17,635 or 19,335 lbs (dependent on parent C54 mark)
Maximum zero fuel – 59,000 or 60,700 lbs (dependent on parent C54 mark)
Maximum Take-off – 73,800 lbs   Maximum landing – 64,170 lbs
Wing loading (at max take-off weight) – 50.5 lb/sq ft
Wing loading (at max landing weight) – 43.9 lb/sq ft

Powerplants four Pratt & Whitney Twin Wasp R2000-7M2 each rated at 1450 bhp take-off power (but see test chapters) at 2700 rpm. No water injection.

Propellers Hamilton Standard 3-blade Hydromatic, 13' 1" diameter, fully feathering, no reversal, low-pitch seating 24°, high pitch 93°, constant speed range 24°– 40°

Performance Level speeds at 50000 lbs gross weight with 3 engines at constant operation
    at 650 bhp/engine – 177 mph IAS at sea level, 158 mph IAS at 10,000 ft
    at 700 bhp/engine – 184 mph IAS at sea level, 168 mph IAS at 10,000 ft
    at 750 bhp/engine – 192 mph IAS at sea level, 176 mph IAS at 10,000 ft

Level speeds at 50000 lbs gross weight with all engines at constant operation
    at 650 bhp/engine – 208 mph IAS at sea level, 193 mph IAS at 10000 ft
    at 675 bhp/engine – 212 mph IAS at sea level, 197 mph IAS at 10000 ft
    at 750 bhp/engine – 216 mph IAS at sea level, 201 mph IAS at 10000 ft.

Maximum speed (Vne) – 217 kts IAS, Normal operating speed (Vno) – 185 kts IAS
Automatic pilot limit speed – 181 kts IAS   Approach speed – 93 kts IAS
Economical cruising speed – 188 kts IAS at 10000 ft   Climb speed – 129 kts IAS

Performance (continued)

Manoeuvring speed (Va) at maximum take-off weight – 162 kts IAS

Wing flaps fully extended (45°) speed (Vfe) – 133 kts IAS

Landing gear extended speed (Vlo) – 156 kts IAS

Take-off to 50 feet (B.C.A.R. max take-off weight, all engines operating)

At I.S.A. at sea level – 4200 ft

At I.S.A. + 15°C at sea level – 5100 ft

At I.S.A. at 5000 ft – 5730 ft

(to meet F.A.A. certification standard: I.S.A., sea level, at F.A.A. max take-off weight of 72,900 lbs, balanced field length – 5,060 ft)

Landing distance from 50 feet (B.C.A.R. max landing weight)

At I.S.A. at sea level –3120 ft

(to meet F.A.A. certification standard: I.S.A., sea level, at F.A.A. max landing weight of 63,800 lbs, landing distance – 2665 ft)

Range – still air, no reserve, I.S.A. with max fuel (3000 Imperial gallons) with 10000 lbs payload, 184 kts at 10,000 ft – 3,000 nautical miles

– still air, no reserve, I.S.A. with max payload, 184 kts at 10,000 ft

– 2000 nautical miles (both ranges are from take-off to landing)

Fuel system   varies with particular C54/DC4 type converted, but any combination of six integral tanks in outer wings, two auxiliary bag tanks in inner wings or fuselage tankage could be encountered. (purchasing operators required their Carvair systems to be compatible with other C54 or DC4 types already in company use). Maximum speed for fuel jettisoning – 191 kts IAS.
Engine-driven fuel pumps with tank booster pumps as standby.
Fuel consumption – 175 Imperial gallons per hour (maximum).

Structure   semi-monocoque fuselage, three-spar fail-safe wing.
All flying controls cable operated, one-piece aileron with trim tab on starboard only, both elevators and rudder have a trim tab.
Flaps are single-slotted, no speed brakes fitted.

Undercarriage   twin-wheeled main legs retract forward into inboard engine nacelles, single nosewheel retracts forward partly into fuselage line and is covered by two doors.
Nosewheel steering effective through 45° either side of centreline.
Main undercarriage track – 24' 8"
Nose to main footprint – 27' 4½"
Emergency free-fall system fitted.
Hydraulic pressure system at 3000 lb/in^2 for operation of undercarriage also serves flaps, cowling gills, wheel brakes and nosewheel steering.
Tyre pressures, main wheels – 70 lb/in^2, nosewheel – 55 lb/in^2.

De-icing system   pulsating rubber sleeve on leading edges of wing, tailplane and fin, with rubber overshoes and liquid de-icing via slinger ring for propellors.

Electric system   four engine-driven 6 kW generators for 28-volt DC system with standby batteries rated at 88 Amp-hour. Original C54/DC4 generating system has been reused with revisions to the bus-bar distribution layout.

Air conditioning and heating   each crew position and row of passenger seats has a cold air louvre. The flight deck and passenger areas are served by distribution from a 100,000 BthU combustion heater. (see relevant chapters in text relating to certain conversions which were further modified by an increase in the heating system capacity to cope with the Canadian climate)

Appendix 2

Douglas DC4/C54

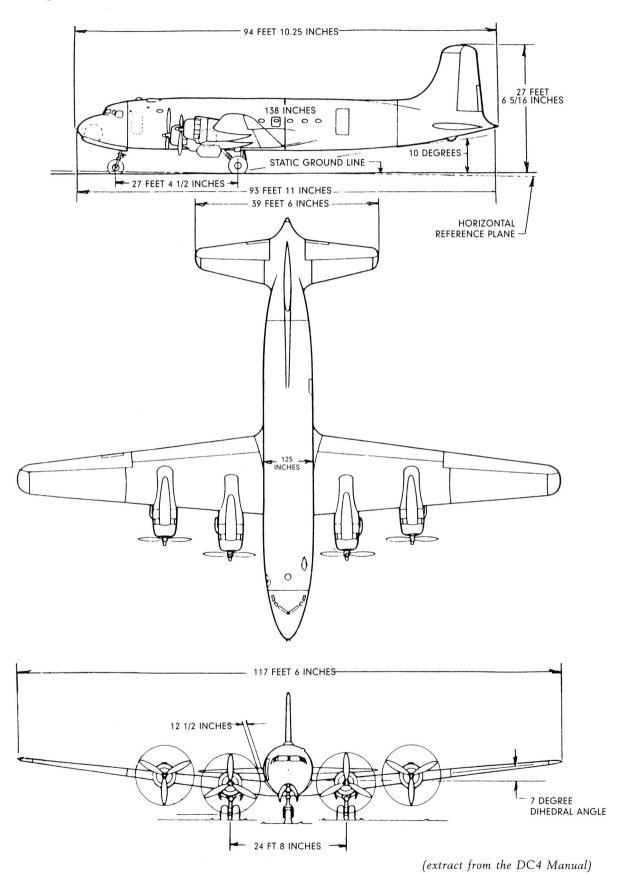

94 FEET 10.25 INCHES

27 FEET
6 5/16 INCHES

138 INCHES

10 DEGREES

STATIC GROUND LINE

27 FEET 4 1/2 INCHES

93 FEET 11 INCHES

39 FEET 6 INCHES

HORIZONTAL
REFERENCE PLANE

125
INCHES

117 FEET 6 INCHES

12 1/2 INCHES

7 DEGREE
DIHEDRAL ANGLE

24 FT 8 INCHES

(extract from the DC4 Manual)

Aviation Traders ATL98 Carvair

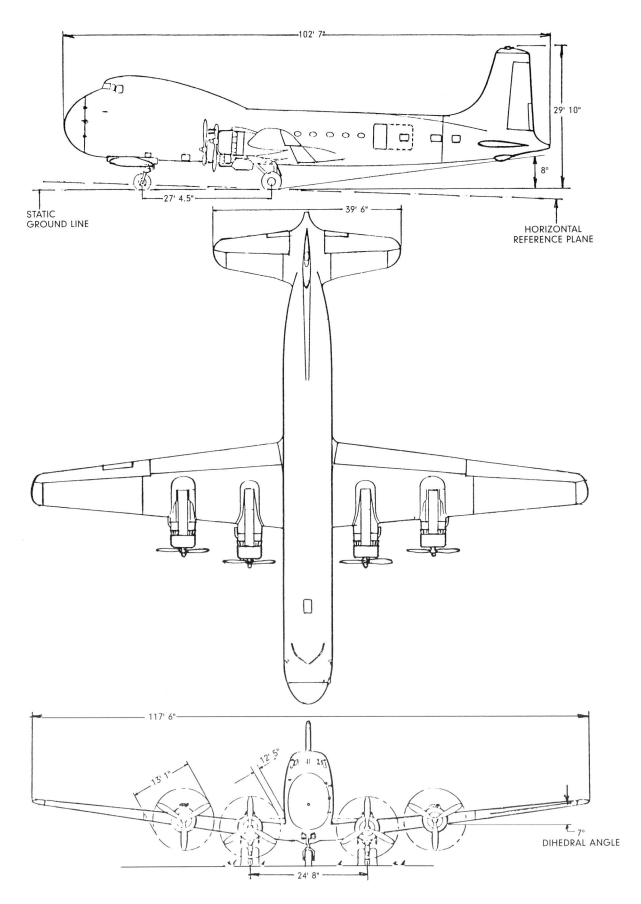

(extract from the Carvair Maintenance Manual)

Proposed Dart Carvair

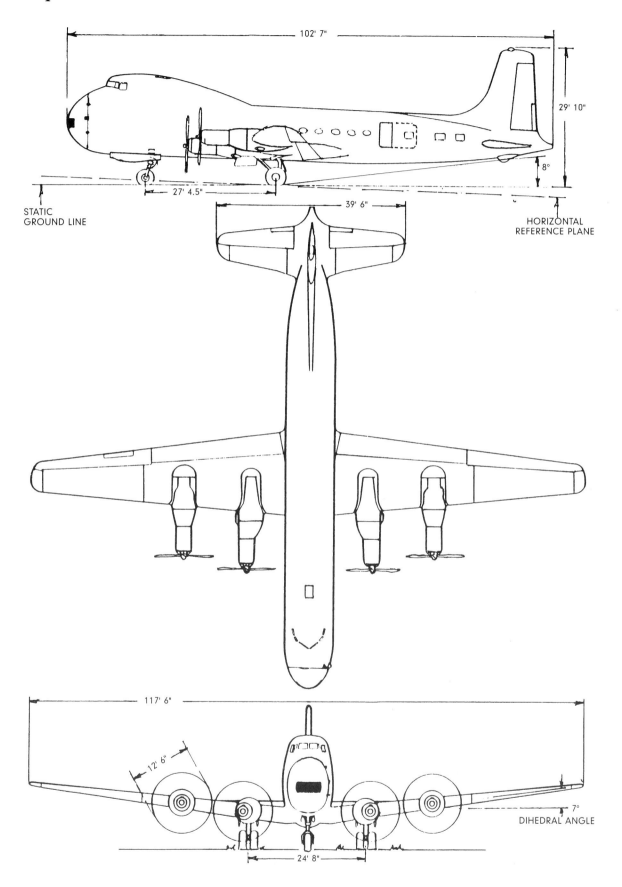

102' 7"

29' 10"

8°

STATIC
GROUND LINE

27' 4.5"

39' 6"

HORIZONTAL
REFERENCE PLANE

117' 6"

12' 6"

7°
DIHEDRAL ANGLE

24' 8"

(courtesy Aviation Traders Engineering Ltd)

Appendix 3

Carvair operators 1961-77

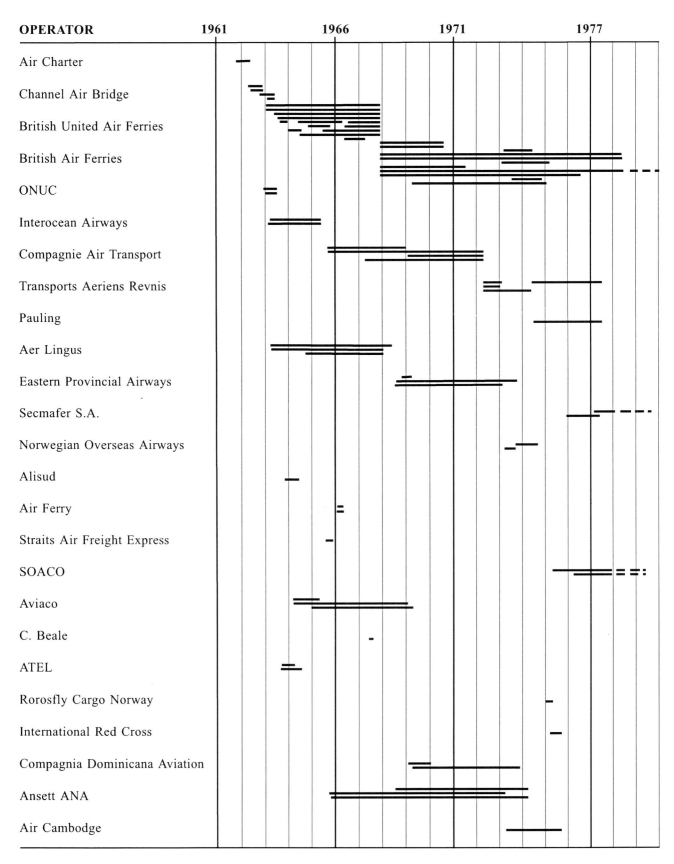

OPERATOR	1961	1966	1971	1977
Air Charter				
Channel Air Bridge				
British United Air Ferries				
British Air Ferries				
ONUC				
Interocean Airways				
Compagnie Air Transport				
Transports Aeriens Revnis				
Pauling				
Aer Lingus				
Eastern Provincial Airways				
Secmafer S.A.				
Norwegian Overseas Airways				
Alisud				
Air Ferry				
Straits Air Freight Express				
SOACO				
Aviaco				
C. Beale				
ATEL				
Rorosfly Cargo Norway				
International Red Cross				
Compagnia Dominicana Aviation				
Ansett ANA				
Air Cambodge				

NOTE: the number of bars against each operator indicates the number of aircraft on charge.

Appendix 4
Company insignia (not depicted elsewhere)

LX-IOH at Stansted carrying Interocean Airways colours

EC-AVD undergoing fuel flow tests at Stansted for the Aviaco lease, before being re-registered as EC-WVD.

(Above)G-ASKG at Stansted at the start of the lease to Alisud, whilst still carrying 'Channel Bridge' above the blue winged dolphin, and (below) at Brazzaville on lease to Air Ferry

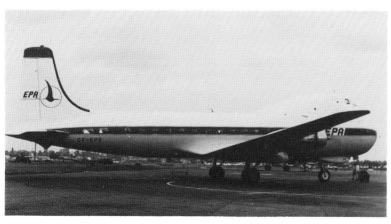

CF-EPV at Southend after respraying in EPA colours.

Appendix 5 – *Typical Carvair vehicle-ferry loadsheet*

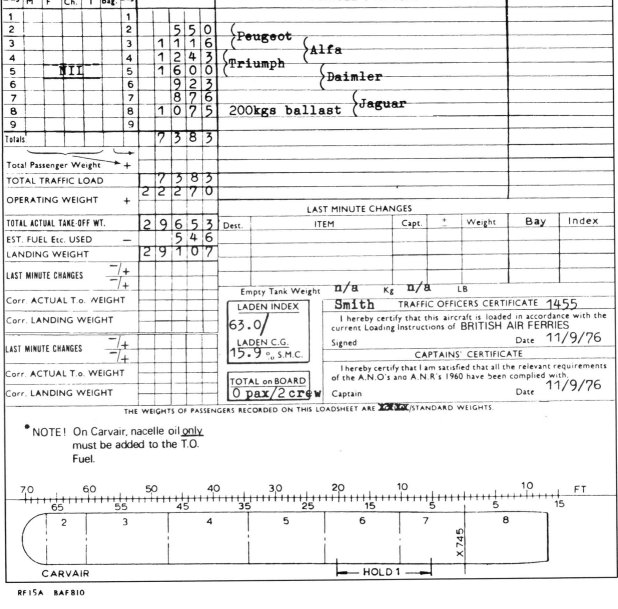

LOADSHEET

BRITISH AIR FERRIES LTD.

ALL WEIGHTS IN KILOS

From SEN	To LTQ	Date 11/9/76	Flight No. VF730X	A/c Type ATL98	A/c Reg. G-ASDC

| A.PS. Weight and Index as Condition No. **DC.FRT.CF** | WEIGHT 1 9 5 2 1 | – INDEX + 77.05 | Airfield Temp. 16°c | | | Captain Rosser + 01 |

Radio rack — INDEX 4

	WEIGHT	INDEX		MAX. Z.F.W.	R.T.O.W.	R.L.W.
ADJUSTED A.P.S. WEIGHT & INDEX	1 9 5 2 5	77.05	MAXIMUM WEIGHTS FOR →	2 7 4 4 3		2 9 1 0 7
T.O. Fuel 830 Galls + Oil 80	2 5 0 0			2 5 0 0 Est.Trip Fuel ↓203 USG		5 4 6
F'wd Crew						
Rear Crew			MAXIMUM ALLOWED T.O. WEIGHT lowest of 1, 2 or 3	¹2 9 9 4 3	²³ 3 4 7 5	³2 9 6 5 3
Crew Baggage						
F'wd Catering		8				
Aft Catering			OPERATING WEIGHT			2 2 2 7 0
Water-Meth. nets Galls.	2 2					
Flight Spares + M/W	2 1 5					
OPERATING WEIGHT	2 2 2 7 0		ALLOWED TRAFFIC LOAD			7 3 8 3

Bay	No. of Pax. M	F	Ch.	I	Cab. Bag.	Bay	TOTAL	VEHICLE / FREIGHT	REMARKS
1						1			
2						2	5 5 0	Peugeot	
3						3	1 1 1 6	Alfa	
4						4	1 2 4 3	Triumph	
5	NIL					5	1 6 0 0	Daimler	
6						6	9 2 3		
7						7	8 7 6	Jaguar	
8						8	1 0 7 5	200kgs ballast	
9						9			
Totals							7 3 8 3		

Total Passenger Weight → +

TOTAL TRAFFIC LOAD	7 3 8 3
OPERATING WEIGHT +	2 2 2 7 0
TOTAL ACTUAL TAKE-OFF WT.	2 9 6 5 3
EST. FUEL Etc. USED –	5 4 6
LANDING WEIGHT	2 9 1 0 7
LAST MINUTE CHANGES –/+ –/+	
Corr. ACTUAL T.o. WEIGHT	
Corr. LANDING WEIGHT	
LAST MINUTE CHANGES –/+ –/+	
Corr. ACTUAL T.o. WEIGHT	
Corr. LANDING WEIGHT	

LAST MINUTE CHANGES

Dest.	ITEM	Capt.	±	Weight	Bay	Index

Empty Tank Weight n/a Kg n/a LB

LADEN INDEX 63.0/

LADEN C.G. 15.9 % S.M.C.

TOTAL on BOARD 0 pax/2 crew

Smith TRAFFIC OFFICERS CERTIFICATE 1455

I hereby certify that this aircraft is loaded in accordance with the current Loading Instructions of BRITISH AIR FERRIES

Signed   Date 11/9/76

CAPTAINS' CERTIFICATE

I hereby certify that I am satisfied that all the relevant requirements of the A.N.O's and A.N.R's 1960 have been complied with.

Captain   Date 11/9/76

THE WEIGHTS OF PASSENGERS RECORDED ON THIS LOADSHEET ARE ACTUAL/STANDARD WEIGHTS.

* NOTE! On Carvair, nacelle oil <u>only</u> must be added to the T.O. Fuel.

RF 15A   BAF 810

Appendix 6 – Histories of aircraft converted to Carvair

A/C Ref	Aviation Traders Construction No.	ATL98/-----/M	Douglas Model & Sub-type	C54B-1-DC
M	Douglas Original Construction No.	10480	Delivery Date (Ex Works)	21.12.44

REGN	NAME	OWNER/OPERATOR	FROM	TO	REMARKS
42-72375					Built at Chicago. To Santa Monica 5.8.46, converted no. 67
NC90862		Santa Fe Skyways			Del 15.1.47. Used in cargo role.
PH-TEZ	Zeeland	KLM			On charge 24.5.48
PH-DBZ		KLM	29. 3.54		Re-registered. RTP 1958
				20. 4.59	Disposed of for scrap at Schipol
		Aviation Traders Engineering Ltd.	Dec. 1959		Front fuselage only to Southend for ATL98 programme design layout and spares recovery

A/C Ref	Aviation Traders Construction No.	ATL98/10528/1	Douglas Model & Sub-type	C54B-1-DC
1	Douglas Original Construction No.	10528	Delivery Date (Ex Works)	22.1.45

REGN	NAME	OWNER/OPERATOR	FROM	TO	REMARKS
42-72423					Built at Chicago
NC88723					
N59952		Braniff Airways Inc.		May 1953	dam Love Field, Dallas 15.5.53
		E.J. Daly (World A/w)	June 1953	31. 1.55	
		Richard R. Riss			(leased) op as World Airways
G-ANYB	Atalanta	Air Charter Ltd	31. 1.55	8. 1.62	Purchased from Braniff Airways, del to Stansted via New York and Shannon
			3.10.60	20. 6.61	Conv to ATL98 (Southend)
				13. 5.61	Rollout
				21. 6.61	First flight (in CAB livery)
		Air Charter Ltd	23. 7.61	10.61	dam on ground at Southend
G-ANYB	Golden Gate Bridge	Channel Air Bridge	8. 1.62	16. 7.62	Del 16.2.62 (Inaugural service to Ostende same day)
		British United Air Ferries	16. 7.62	30. 9.67	Last flight 5.3.67 (Southend-Lydd for open storage/spares recovery)
		British Air Ferries	30. 9.67	26. 8.70	RTP 26.8.70. Airframe ss

A/C Ref	Aviation Traders Construction No.	ATL98/10311/2	Douglas Model & Sub-type	C54A-10-DC
2	Douglas Original Construction No.	10311	Delivery Date (Ex Works)	27.5.44

REGN	NAME	OWNER/OPERATOR	FROM	TO	REMARKS
42-72206					Built at Chicago
N57670		California Eastern Aviation Inc			On charge May 1952
		Transocean Airlines			
		Resort Airlines Inc		19 7.61	On official contract – Logair
G-ARSD		Channel Air Bridge	14. 7.61	–	Del from store at Oakland, Calif to Stansted July 1961
			18. 7.61	25. 3.62	Conv to ATL98 (Stansted)
				25. 3.62	First flight (Stansted-Southend)
G-ARSD	Chelsea Bridge	Channel Air Bridge	–	16. 7.62	Del 2.4.62
		British United Air Ferries	16. 7.62	30. 9.67	
		British Air Ferries	30. 9.67	26. 8.70	Last flight 4.10.67 (Southend-Lydd for open storage/spares recovery)
				26. 8.70	RTP. Airframe ss

A/C Ref	Aviation Traders Construction No.	ATL98/18339/3		Douglas Model & Sub-type	C54B-5-DO
3	Douglas Original Construction No.	18339		Delivery Date (Ex Works)	10.7.44

REGN	NAME	OWNER/OPERATOR	FROM	TO	REMARKS
43-17139					Built at Orlando
N88709		Braniff Airways Inc.	Nov 1945		
		Northwest Airlines Incorporated	Oct 1950		(leased)
		Transocean Airlines Incorporated			(sub-leased) dam in ground fire at Keflavlik, Iceland 10/6/54
		Resort Airlines Inc	Oct 1954	19.7.61	On official contract – Logair
G-ARSF		Channel Air Bridge	17. 7.61	–	Del from store at Oakland, Calif to Stansted July 1961
			22. 7.61	28. 6.62 28. 6.62	Conv to ATL98 (Stansted) First flight
G-ARSF	Pont da L'Europe	Channel Air Bridge	–	5. 2.63	Del 7.7.62 Cr at Rotterdam, Neth 28.12.62 wreck recovered to England, RTP w/o 5.2.63

A/C Ref	Aviation Traders Construction No.	ATL98/10338/4		Douglas Model & Sub-type	C54A-10-DC
4	Douglas Original Construction No.	10338		Delivery Date (Ex Works)	30.6.44

REGN	NAME	OWNER/OPERATOR	FROM	TO	REMARKS
42-72233					Built at Chicago
N65142		Braniff Airways Inc	Nov 1945		
		Resort Airlines Inc	Nov 1954	17. 7.61	On official contract – Logair
		Slick Airways Inc			On charge 1.7.59 (believed leased)
G-ARSH		Channel Air Bridge	17. 7.61	4. 9.62	Del from store at Oakland, Calif to Stansted July 1961
			27. 7.61	5. 9.62	Conv to ATL98 (Stansted), wider door cill installed on line
G-41-2				5. 9.62	First flight (Stansted-Southend)
N9758F		United Nations Air Operations in the Congo	5.10.62	27. 2.63	Del 24.9.62. Operated on charter from Intercontinental U.S. Inc
LX-IOH		Interocean Airways S.A.	18.12.62	30. 4.65 28. 4.65	(Leased) owned by U.S. Transport Corporation, Dower, Delaware Returned to Stansted
F-BMHU	Henri de Montal	Compagnie Air Transport	24. 6.65	19.12.68	Del 19.6.65 cr near Karachi, Pakistan 8.3.67 ss locally, w/o 19.12.68

A/C Ref	Aviation Traders Construction No.	ATL98/10365/5		Douglas Model & Sub-type	C54A-15-DC
5	Douglas Original Construction No.	10365		Delivery Date (Ex Works)	3.8.44

REGN	NAME	OWNER/OPERATOR	FROM	TO	REMARKS
42-72260					Built at Chicago
BU 50843		United States Navy			
NC57777		Matson Navigation Company			
VP-CBD		Air Ceylon – Dept of Civil Aviation	3. 2.49		
CY-ACA			27. 9.50		
VH-INY	Laxapana	ANA	16. 3.51		

continued on next page

REGN	NAME	OWNER/OPERATOR	FROM	TO	REMARKS
N5520V		T.C.A.C.	29. 4.58		(initially leased)
		Seven Seas Airlines			(leased) based at Luxembourg
D-ADAL		Transavia	24..5.58		Based at Dusseldorf
		L.T.U.	7. 2.59		Based at Cologne
G-AREK		Air Charter Ltd.	20. 9.60	4.9.62	Del from Cologne to Stansted on 18.8.60, handed over 28.8.60
			27.12.61	2.11.62	Conv to ATL98 (Stansted), wider door cill installed on line
				2.11.62	First flight
N9757F		United Nations Air Operations in the Congo	23.11.62	17. 2.63	Del 20.11.62. Operated on charter from Intercontinental U.S. Inc
LX-IOG		Interocean Airways S.A.	5.12.62	30. 4.65	(leased) owned by Winston Factors Inc, New York
				28. 4.65	Returned to Stansted
F-BMHV	Commandant Max Guedjt	Compagnie Air Transport	24. 6.65	17. 4.72	Del 31.5.65. Wfu 1970 into open storage with Air Fret at Nimes
		British Air Ferries	11. 3.72		(on loan)
		*T.A.R.	17. 4.72	23. 2.73	(*Société de Transports Aeriens Revnis)
G-AREK	Porky Pete	British Air Ferries	23. 2.73	13. 6.74	(on lease from T.A.R.)
G-AREK		Pauling (Middle East) Ltd.	13. 6.74	14. 6.77	Signed over to Pauling (Middle East) Ltd 15.5.74, del 20.6.74
			Feb 1976		o/o/s at Southend
F-BCYL		Secmafer S.A.	24. 6.77	–	(beyond scope of this book)

A/C Ref 6	Aviation Traders Construction No.	ATL98/7480/6		Douglas Model & Sub-type	C54A-5-DO
	Douglas Original Construction No.	7480		Delivery Date (Ex Works)	11.4.44

REGN	NAME	OWNER/OPERATOR	FROM	TO	REMARKS
42-107461					Built at Orlando
NC90431	Flagship Philadelphia	American			
		Airplane Enterprises	24. 9.54		(initially leased)
YV-C-AVH		Avensa			
N75298		Resort Airlines Inc		7. 6.62	
		World Airways Inc	1. 7.60	27. 6.61	(leased)
					On official contract – Logair
G-ARZV		Channel Air Bridge	8. 6.62	–	Del from store at Oakland, Calif to Stansted 14.6.62
			14. 6.62	20.12.62	Conv to ATL98 (Stansted), elevated control runs installed on line
				21.12.62	First flight
		Channel Air Bridge	–	2. 1.63	
EI-AMP	Ailbhe (stb) St Albert (port)	Aer Lingus – Irish International	5. 2.63	29. 5.68	Del to Dublin 14.3.63 dam at Stansted 8.1.64, repaired and RTS. dam by in-flight engine fire near Dublin 2.5.68, repaired and RTS
				1. 7.68	To Southend for systems upgrading
CF-EPX		Eastern Provincial Airways (1963) Ltd.	24. 7.68	31. 1.69	Del to Gander 5.7.68 Cr at Twin Falls, Newfoundland 28.9.68, DBR and w/o 31.1.69

A/C Ref	Aviation Traders Construction No.	ATL98/10273/7		Douglas Model & Sub-type		C54A-1-DC
7	Douglas Original Construction No.	10273		Delivery Date (Ex Works)		6.11.43

REGN	NAME	OWNER/OPERATOR	FROM	TO	REMARKS
42-72168					Built at Chicago
		Arrow Airlines			
N54373	Wake Island Airtrader	Seaboard & Western Airlines	19. 9.53		To Seaboard World Airlines 1961, carried N54373V for a period
LX-BNG		United Nations	20.3.61	5. 4.61	On contract for Congo operations Owned by Marshall Landy of Miami, Florida since 3.3.61 Registration alludes to initials of one company director Benjamin Nathaniel Goldberg
		Interocean Airways S.A.	5. 4.61	10.10.62	(leased)
			17. 8.62	17. 8.62 19. 3.63 22. 3.63	Del from Luxembourg to Stansted Conv to ATL98 (Stansted) First flight
G-ASDC	Pont du Rhin	British United Air Ferries	11. 1.63	30. 9.67	Del 26.3.63
	Big Louie	British Air Ferries	30. 9.67	11. 2.75	dam at Rotterdam, Neth 17.2.70 repaired and RTS
	Plain Jane	British Air Ferries	11. 2.75	10. 3.79	Conv to cargo freighter

A/C Ref	Aviation Traders Construction No.	ATL98/10448/8		Douglas Model & Sub-type		C54B-1-DC
8	Douglas Original Construction No.	10448		Delivery Date (Ex Works)		15.11.44

REGN	NAME	OWNER/OPERATOR	FROM	TO	REMARKS
42-72343					Built at Chicago.
N88819		T.C.A.C.			Op as North American
		Resort Airlines Inc			
		World Airways Inc	2. 7.60	29. 6.61	(leased)
				19. 7.61	On Official contract – Logair
					Del from store at Oakland, Calif to Stansted 22.10.62
		Slick Airways Inc		14.11.62	(leased)
			23.10.62	19. 4.63	Conv to ATL98 (Stansted), elevated control runs installed on line
				19. 4.63	First flight (Stansted-Southend)
EI-AMR	Larfhlaith (stb) St. Jarlath (port)	Aer Lingus – Irish International	5. 2.63	16. 2.68	Del to Dublin 29.4.63
				22. 5.68	To Southend for systems upgrading
CF-EPV		Eastern Provincial Airways (1963) Ltd	4. 7.68	3.10.73	Del to Gander 24.5.68 o/o/s Oct 1969-Nov 1970 dam Gander 3.5.72, repaired, RTS
				21. 9.73	del to Southend via Gander and Keflavlik for servicing
		Norwegian Overseas Airways	3.10.73	9. 9.74	(leased) owned by R.C.S. Graham of Prince Rupert, B.C. Impounded at Southend
				1978	RTP, nose door to static G-AOFW, nose to Suffolk museum, noseleg to Essex museum, remainder ss.

A/C Ref	Aviation Traders Construction No.	ATL98/27249/9		Douglas Model & Sub-type		C54B-20-DO
9	Douglas Original Construction No.	27249		Delivery Date (Ex Works)		11.1.45

REGN	NAME	OWNER/OPERATOR	FROM	TO	REMARKS
42-9023					Built at Orlando
				2.12.45	To El Segundo, converted no. 10
N88816		Western Air Lines			Del 2.7.46
XA-MAA		Guest Aerovias			On charge 18.12.56
HP-268		Aerovias de Panama	Sep 1957		(leased)
CP-682		Lloyd Aereo Boliviano S.A.	1. 4.60		(leased)
				30. 1.62	Del Gander to Paris as CP-682
N9326R		Babb Co. Ltd	late 1961	27. 3.63	Del Paris to Stansted 26.10.62
			29.10.62	8. 6.63	Conv to ATL98 (Stansted)
				8. 6.63	First flight
G-ASHZ	Maasbrug	British United Air Ferries	6. 5.63	30. 9.67	Del 15.6.63
		British Air Ferries	30. 9.67	Jul 1977	
	Fat Annie	British Air Ferries	Jul 1977	10. 3.79	Conv to cargo freighter

A/C Ref	Aviation Traders Construction No.	ATL98/10382/10		Douglas Model & Sub-type		C54A-15-DC
10	Douglas Original Construction No.	10382		Delivery Date (Ex Works)		24.8.44

REGN	NAME	OWNER/OPERATOR	FROM	TO	REMARKS
42-72277		USAF	24. 8.44		Built at Chicago
LN-HAU	Norse Trader	Braathens	13. 3.47	16.11.50	To Braathens South American and Far East Transport 1949
N1221V		Trans Caribbean Airways	16.11.50		
N1221V	Oslo Airtrader Delhi Airtrader	Seaboard & Western Airlines		1961	(leased) Renamed Seaboard World Airlines
LX-BBP		United Nations	18. 3.61	27. 3.61	On contract for Congo operations owned by Lewmar Corporation of Miami, Florida. Registration alludes to initials of one company director Bernard Benjamin Peck
		Interocean Airways S.A.	27. 3.61	10.10.62	(leased)
				11.11.62	Del from Luxembourg to Stansted
			11.12.62	29. 7.63	Conv to ATL98 (Stansted)
				29. 7.63	First flight
G-ASKG	Channel Bridge	British United Air Ferries	12. 7.63	6. 8.63	No service use
		*Alisud	6. 8.63	25 .2.64	(leased) del to Naples 8.8.63 (*Compagnia Aerea Meridionale)
		British United Air Ferries	25. 3.64	28.12.65	Entered service 25.3.64
		Air Ferry Ltd.	28.12.65	11. 3.66	(leased) del via Malta to Dar-es-Salaam 28.12.65
		British United Air Ferries	11. 3.66	18. 3.69	Re-entered service 25. 3.66
F-BRPT		Compagnie Air Transport	18. 3.69	17. 4.72	del 3.3.69 Wfu at Le Touquet 1970 for open storage with Air Fret at Nimes
		British Air Ferries	11. 3.72	–	(on loan)
F-BRPT		*T.A.R.	17. 4.72	26. 3.73	(*Société de Transports Aeriens Reunis)
G-ASKG	Big Joe	British Air Ferries	26. 3.73	25. 2.75	
TR-LUP	Big Joe	*SOACO of Libreville	25. 2.75	–	Del 25.2,.75 as G-ASKG (*Société Anonyme de Construction) (beyond the scope of this book)

A/C Ref	Aviation Traders Construction No.		ATL98/18333/11	Douglas Model & Sub-type		C54B-5-DO
11	Douglas Original Construction No.		18333	Delivery Date (Ex Works)		24.8.44

REGN	NAME	OWNER/OPERATOR	FROM	TO	REMARKS
43-17133					Built at Orlando
				26.12.45	To Santa Monica. conv no. 34
N37477		Delta Air Lines Inc			Del 27.4.46
		J. Lewis			Painted 'North American Airlines'
		Trans American Airlines			
		T.C.A.C.			
D-ANET		L.T.U.		Apr 1958	Intended but not used
G-APNH		Independent Air Travel Ltd	17. 6.58	11. 9.59	Based at Hurn
		Blue Air Ltd	15.10.59	9.11.59	
		Astraeus Ltd	8. 3.60	23. 3.60	
		Air Charter Ltd	25. 3.60	24. 8.64	Bad debt claim
			1.12.62	4. 1.65 / 4. 1.65	Conv to ATL98 (Southend) / First flight
	Menai Bridge	British United Air Ferries	27. 8.64	30. 9.67	Del 10.1.65
	Menai Bridge	Straits Air Freight Express	16.10.65	1.12.65	(chartered) SAFE titles not used
	Menai Bridge	Air Ferry Ltd			(leased) on charge Feb 1966
		British Air Ferries	30. 9.67	2. 6.71	Cr Le Touquet 18.3.71 Airframe ss, engines and propellers returned to United Kingdom w/o 2.6.71

A/C Ref	Aviation Traders Construction No.		ATL98/10351/12	Douglas Model & Sub-type		C54A-15-DC
12	Douglas Original Construction No.		10351	Delivery Date (Ex Works)		15.7.44

REGN	NAME	OWNER/OPERATOR	FROM	TO	REMARKS
43-72246					Built at Chicago
				17. 6.46	To El Segundo, conv no. 25
N88919	Clipper Panama Clipper Talisman	Pan American Airlines			
		T.C.A.C.			
N1436V		California Eastern Aviation Inc			
I-DALV	Citta da Napoli	Alitalia	21. 4.50	9.12.55	
G-AOFW	Jason	Air Charter Ltd.	9.12.55	3.10.63	Del 11.12.55 to Hanover from Rome for overhaul, then to Berlin
			23. 4.63	7.10.56 / 11. 2.64 / 11. 2.64	Del to Southend from Berlin Conv to ATL98 (Stansted) First flight
		British United Air Ferries	9.10.63	17. 3.64	
EC-AVD		Aviaco	18. 3.64	6. 3.65	(leased) del 18.4.64 from Stansted as EC-WVD
EC-AVD				16.11.64	Returned to UK
G-AOFW		British United Air Ferries	8. 3.65	30. 9.67	Del 3.4.65
			7. 2.67	29. 4.69	To Lydd for open storage
		British Air Ferries	30. 9.67	29. 4.69	
	Big John	British Air Ferries	29. 4.69	8.75	
	Startrukkin		8.75		(leased)
		British Air Ferries	8.75	1983 / 8.83	To Southend for open storage 1977 ss and broken up at Southend

A/C Ref	Aviation Traders Construction No.		ATL98/3058/13		Douglas Model & Sub-type		C54A-5-DO
13	Douglas Original Construction No.		3058		Delivery Date (Ex Works)		8.2.43

REGN	NAME	OWNER/OPERATOR	FROM	TO	REMARKS
41-37272					Built at Orlando
					Sold by C.A.A. as unairworthy
NC79000	721	Eastern Air Lines Inc			On charge 11.4.51
		Aero Leases Inc			On charge May 1955 Company formed by principals of North American and California Eastern
		Grimley Engineering	6.55		(leased) owned first by Northwest, then California Eastern
		Transocean Air Lines Incorporated	28. 2.58		(leased) one flight only
		World Airways Inc			On charge 1959
		Global Aviation			
		California Airmotive			
		President Airlines Inc			(leased) del 14.10.60
D-ADEM		Continentale D.L.			On charge May 1961
		Kunderkreditbank Essen			Bad debt claim (receivers for Continentale D.L.)
G-ASKN		Aviation Traders Engineering Ltd	22. 7.63	–	
G-ASKN				25. 7.63	Del to Southend from Hamburg
			25. 7.63	8. 2.64	Conv to ATL98 (Stansted), elevated control runs installed on line
				8. 2.64	First flight
		Aviation Traders Engineering Ltd.	–	28. 2.64	
	Pont D'Avignon	British United Air Ferries	2. 3.64	30. 9.67	Del 26. 3.64
		Colin Beale	8.67	8.67	(leased) op as CB Flying Showcases
	Big Bill	British Air Ferries	30. 9.67	10. 6.76	
TR-LWP	Big Bill	SOACO of Libreville	10. 6.76	–	Del to Libreville from Southend (beyond the scope of this book)

A/C Ref	Aviation Traders Construction No.		ATL98/10458/14		Douglas Model & Sub-type		C54B-1-DC
14	Douglas Original Construction No.		10458		Delivery Date (Ex Works)		27.11.44

REGN	NAME	OWNER/OPERATOR	FROM	TO	REMARKS
42-72353					Built at Chicago
				18. 1.46	To El Segundo, conv no. 17
N88721		Western Air Lines			Del 14.9.46
OO-SBO		Sobelair	15. 2.56		
		Sabena	25. 3.56		(leased) ret to Sobelair on expiry
F-BHVR		U.A.T.	25.11.56	15. 3.57	(leased) ret to Sobelair on expiry
OO-SBO		Sabena	15. 3.57	31.10.59	(leased)
D-ANEK		Continentale D.L.	18. 4.60		
		Mercard & Co. Hamburg			Bad debt claim (receivers for Continentale D.L.
G-ASKD		Aviation Traders Engineering Ltd.	9. 7.63	–	
G-ASKD				31. 7.63	Del to Southend from Hamburg

continued on next page

A/C Ref 14 continued

REGN	NAME	OWNER/OPERATOR	FROM	TO	REMARKS
			31. 7.63	17. 4.64	Conv to ATL98 (Stansted), elevated control runs installed on line
				17. 4.64	First flight
		Aviation Traders Engineering Ltd.	–	9. 6.64	
EI-ANJ	Seanan (stb) St Senan (port)	Aer Lingus – Irish International	17.11.64	16. 2.68	Del to Dublin 24.4.64
				2. 6.68	To Southend for systems upgrading
CF-EPW		Eastern Provincial Airways (1963) Ltd	4. 7.68 10.69	17. 4.73 11.70	Del to Gander 6.6.68 o/o/s at Gander
		Norwegian Overseas Airways	17. 4.73	3. 8.73	(leased) owned by R.C.S. Graham of Prince Rupert, BC
				20. 4.73	dam at Gander, repaired and RTS
				6.73	Del to Southend from Gander
G-ASKD		British Air Ferries	6. 8.73	11.11.74	(sub-lease from NOA)
LN-NAA	Viking North Sea Express	Rorosfly Cargo Norway	28. 1.75	1. 4.75	Del 2.2.75
LN-NAA		International Red Cross	1. 4.75	9.10.75	(leased) a/c left for Far East via Basle and Bahrein but impounded at Bangkok 4.4.75

A/C Ref	Aviation Traders Construction No.		ATL98/27311/15	Douglas Model & Sub-type		C54E-10-DO
15	Douglas Original Construction No.		27311	Delivery Date (Ex Works)		5.4.45

REGN	NAME	OWNER/OPERATOR	FROM	TO	REMARKS
44-9085					Built at Orlando
				, 26.9.45	To Santa Monica, conv no. 2
N88886	Clipper Mandarin	Pan American Airways			Del 14.11.45
	Clipper Frankfurt				
	Clipper Pegasus				
	Clipper Hanover				
OD-ADW		Trans Mediterranean Airways			On charge 12.1.61 at Abu Heida, Lebanon
				11.63	Del to Stansted from Beirut
			8.11.63	23. 3.66	Conv to ATL98 (Stansted)
				23. 3.66	First flight
G-ATRV		British United Air Ferries	7. 3.66	17. 4.67	Del 1.4.66
F-BOSU	President Gamel	Compagnie Air Transport	10. 5.67	17. 4.72	Del 7.5.67 dam by e/f over Sahara 21.11.67 repaired and RTS
				1970	Wfu at Le Touquet
		T.A.R.		17. 4.72	(Société de Transports Aeriens Revnis)
		Air Fret	17. 4.72	?	RTP at Nimes-Garons

A/C Ref	Aviation Traders Construction No.	ATL98/10485/16	Douglas Model & Sub-type	C54B-1-DC
16	Douglas Original Construction No.	10485	Delivery Date (Ex Works)	23.12.44

REGN	NAME	OWNER/OPERATOR	FROM	TO	REMARKS
42-72380					Built at Chicago
NC90417	Flagship Monterey	American			
EC-AEP		Iberia			On charge 1949
		Aviaco		–	(subsidiary of Iberia)
			18. 2.64	15. 2.64	Del to Stansted from Barcelona
				4. 6.64	Conv to ATL98 (Stansted)
				4. 6.64	First flight
EC-AXI		Aviaco	–	20. 2.69	Del 24.6.64 as EC-WXI
HI-168		Cia Dominicana	20. 2.69	21.12.69	Donated as part of an aid scheme
					Cr at Miami 23.6.69. w/o 1.1.70

A/C Ref	Aviation Traders Construction No.	ATL98/18342/17	Douglas Model & Sub-type	C54B-5-DO
17	Douglas Original Construction No.	18342	Delivery Date (Ex Works)	19.7.44

REGN	NAME	OWNER/OPERATOR	FROM	TO	REMARKS
43-17142					Built at Orlando
				7.11.45	To Santa Monica, conv no. 9
N30042	Cargoliner Rainier	United Air Lines			Del 26. 2.46
		Transocean Air Lines Incorporated		29.12.56	On charge, resold October 1959
		Lufthansa			(leased)
		U.S. Transport Corpn			(New York)
		Intercontinental U.S. Inc	8.60	14. 6.62	(leased) owned by U.S. Transport Corpn of New York
LX-IOF		Interocean Airways S.A.	5. 7.62	14. 2.64	(leased) owned by U.S. Transport Corpn of New York
				5. 2.64	Del to Southend from Luxembourg
				6. 2.64	Del to Stansted
			10. 2.64	2. 4.69	Conv to ATL98 (Stansted)
				2. 4.69	First flight
G-AXAI	Fat Albert	British Air Ferries	19. 2.69	29.12.75	Del 5.4.69
F-BBEF		Secmafer S.A.	29.12.75	5. 1.76	Del to Nice 7.1.76 as G-AXAI
G-AXAI		Secmafer S.A.	5. 1.76	27. 1.76	Reregistered on British register
F-BBEF		Secmafer S.A.	27. 1.76	–	(Beyond scope of this book)

A/C Ref	Aviation Traders Construction No.	ATL98/18340/18	Douglas Model & Sub-type	C54B-5-DO
18	Douglas Original Construction No.	18340	Delivery Date (Ex Works)	12.7.44

REGN	NAME	OWNER/OPERATOR	FROM	TO	REMARKS
43-17140					Built at Orlando
NC90403	Flagship Phoenix	American			
EC-AEO	115	Iberia			
EC-AXY		Aviaco		–	(Subsidiary of Iberia)
				5.11.64	Del to Stansted from Barcelona
			5.11.64	12. 3.65	Conv to ATL98 (Stansted)
				12. 3.65	First flight
EC-AZA		Aviaco	–	22. 3.69	Del 26.3.65 as EC-WZA
HI-172		Cia Dominicana	22. 3.69	?	Donated as part of an aid scheme
				12. 1.70	Last flight. Wfu at Santo Domingo
				1975	ss to local restaurant

A/C Ref 19	Aviation Traders Construction No.	ATL98/42927/19		Douglas Model & Sub-type		DC4
	Douglas Original Construction No.	42927		Delivery Date (Ex Works)		17.5.46
REGN	NAME	OWNER/OPERATOR	FROM	TO	REMARKS	
SE-BBD	Monsun	S.I.L.A.				
	Styrbjorn Viking Sigmund	S.A.S./A.B.A.				
JA6008	Zao	Japanese Air Lines			On charge 23.2.54	
VH-INJ		Ansett-ANA	7. 8.63	17. 9.65		
		Airlines of New South Wales			(leased) arr Adelaide 24.2.64	
			17. 5.65	16. 5.65 14. 9.65	Del to Stansted via Southend Conv to ATL98 (Stansted), elevated control runs and widened front loading door cill installed on line	
				14. 9.65	First flight	
VH-INJ		Ansett-ANA	17. 9.65	3. 7.73	Del 23.9.65 o/o/s February 1973	
N33AC	Barb	Air Cambodge	3. 7.73	?	(leased) owned by Munro Aircraft Sales of Mascot Airport, Sydney W/o 1975 due to damage suffered during hostilities at Phnom Penh	

A/C Ref 20	Aviation Traders Construction No.	ATL98/42994/20		Douglas Model & Sub-type		DC4
	Douglas Original Construction No.	42994		Delivery Date (Ex Works)		24.6.46
REGN	NAME	OWNER/OPERATOR	FROM	TO	REMARKS	
LN-IAE		D.N.L.				
	Olav Viking	S.A.S./D.N.L.				
JA6012	Mikasa	Japanese Air Lines			On charge 27.10.56	
HL4003						
VH-INK		Ansett-ANA	21. 2.64	28.10.65	Del 22.2.64	
			26. 6.65	25. 6.65 27.10.65	Del to Stansted via Southend Conv to ATL98 (Stansted), elevated control runs and widened front loading door cill installed on line	
				27.10.65	First flight	
VH-INK		Ansett-ANA	28.10.65	11. 2.74	Del 4.11.65	
		Australian Aircraft Sales Ltd (Djakarta)	11. 2.74	mid 1976	Reported static at Sydney 22.3.75 Reported at Singapore April 1975 Taken off register 25.8.75	
		Dwen Automotive	mid 1976	?	(beyond scope of this book)	

A/C Ref 21	Aviation Traders Construction No.	ATL98/27314/21		Douglas Model & Sub-type		C54E-10-DO
	Douglas Original Construction No.	27314		Delivery Date (Ex Works)		7.4.45
REGN	NAME	OWNER/OPERATOR	FROM	TO	REMARKS	
44-9088			12. 4.45		Built at Orlando	
			14.11.45		To Santa Monica. conv no. 13	
N88881	Clipper Kit Carson Clipper Golden West Clipper Red Rover	Pan American Airways			Del 23.12.45	
JA6015	Amagi	Japanese Air Lines			On charge 15.2.58	
VH-INM		Ansett-ANA	19. 3.65	16. 7.68	Del to Southend 29.2.68	

continued on next page

A/C Ref 21 continued

REGN	NAME	OWNER/OPERATOR	FROM	TO	REMARKS
VH-INM			l. 3.68	12. 7.68 12. 7.68	Conv to ATL98 (Southend) elevated control runs and widened front loading door cill installed on line First flight
		Ansett-ANA	16. 7.68	11. 2.74	Del 19.7.68
		Australian Aircraft Sales Ltd. (Djakarta)	11. 2.74	mid 1976	Static at Sydney 22.3.75 Reported Singapore April 1975 Taken off register 25.8.75
		Dwen Airmotive	mid 1976	?	(beyond scope of this book)

ABBREVIATIONS			
Conv	converted	o/o/s	out of service
Cr	crashed	RTP	reduced to produce
dam	damaged	RTS	returned to service
DBR	damaged beyond repair	ss	sold as scrap
del	delivered	stb	starboard
Inc	Incorporated	Wfu	withdrawn from use
op	operated	w/o	written off

The ultimate dinner party conversation piece. The once-flying, and only, model of Carvair G-ASHZ now hanging from the ceiling in ex-BAF captain Laurie Rowe's dining room.

Bibliography

A History of Aviation in Essex (edited by K. Cole) Pub: RAeS (Southend branch) 1967
Aer Lingus – a history (author unknown)
The Aeroplane magazine
The Aeroplane and Astronautics magazine, February 1962
The Aeroplane and Commercial Aviation News – Air Holdings supplement, January 1965
Aircraft Illustrated magazine (various)
Airfix magazine (various)
Airline Quarterly (various)
Air Pictorial magazine (various)
Air Transport Hulks (Nigel Tomkins) Pub: Airline Publications
Aviation News (various)
Aviation Week and Space Technology (various)
Bristol Aircraft (J.D. Oughton) Pub: Ian Allan
British Air Ferries flight schedules and safety information leaflets
British Civil Aircraft from 1916 (A.J. Jackson) Pub: Putnam
The Bristol 170 (J D Oughton) *Aircraft Illustrated* Feb-May 1967
Carvair maintenance manual (ATEL)
Carvair repair manual (ATEL)
Carvair spare parts manual (ATEL)
Citroën magazine July 1980
The Douglas DC4 & C54 maintenance manuals
The Douglas C54 operators notes
The Douglas C54/DC4 history (Pub: Air Britain)
Flight magazine (various)
Flypast magazine (various)
Lydd Airport visitors book
New Orleans Times, June 1969
Propliner magazine, Summer 1993
Science Reference Library, London
Shell Aviation News No 333, 1966
Daily Sketch newspapers
Southend Evening Echo newspapers

Note – all technical material relating to the ATL 98, or extracted from the Douglas C54 Aircraft manual, is reproduced by permission of Aviation Traders (Engineering) Ltd) with the kind co-operation of FLS Aerospace (UK) Ltd, Long Border Road, Stansted Airport, Bishops Stortford, Hertfordshire CM24 1RE

Photo credits

All photographs depicting the construction and proving stages are from the now-defunct Aviation Traders archives and reproduced with permission of their current custodians.

Many of the 'service' shots are from the collection amassed by John Simms, a long-time and avid Carvair enthusiast, whose work was invaluable to this book. Other sources are duly credited, and thanks are due to all who contributed vital material. The remaining photographs are from the author's collection.

Author's pages

The author, a member of the Airfield Research Group, the British Society of World War One Aero Historians (Cross & Cockade UK), and the Mosquito Aircraft Museum, currently lives in Hertfordshire and works with the Defence Estates Organisation on behalf of the United States 3rd Air Force in the United Kingdom.

Apart from writing on the conversion of a classic type from 'over the pond' he has also flown two other American aeroplane types, these being the Piper PA28 Warrior 2 and Arrow. Seen here in the 492nd Aero Club Squadron hangar at RAF Lakenheath holding a cockpit sidescreen he also has a portion of under-fuselage baggage hold door from Carvair G-AOFW (scrapped at Southend in 1983), as well as some 'cuddly Carvair' beer mats and a tee-shirt on the aircraft walkway. These promotional items appeared as part of a sales drive by BAF in 1975, at a time when BAF's operations on the vehicle-ferry had declined and the emphasis was on the carriage of various other types of payload, the central logo being a cartoon Carvair with bent wings, embracing passengers on one side, and freight items on the other.   (Merlin Morgan photo)

Still available from Forward Airfield Research Publishing:

Fields of the First

(A history of aircraft landing grounds in Essex used during the First World War)

by Paul A. Doyle

A history of all 31 sites used by the three services during the Great War is complemented by period maps and an aerial photograph of each site as it is now. Further chapters cover the Air Defence of Great Britain, operational aids, surviving buildings from the Great War, plus Royal Flying Corps and German airship memorials.

Appendices cover aircraft patrol lines, operational period for landing grounds, organisation of Home Defence wings and squadrons, ground signals, plans of the major Flight Stations, details of aircraft hangars and sheds used, the cost of aircraft and engines, and a complete listing for personnel and equipment numbers at the Flight Stations.

120 pp, A4 size, softback, laminated cover, illustrated with 52 black and white photographs plus many maps and drawings..

(Highly commended in the 1997 Essex Book Awards)

£15.00 (by post in UK)

Please use reference ISBN 0 9525624 1 3 when ordering through booksellers

Also still available:

Where the Lysanders where . . .

(the story of Sawbridgeworth's airfields)

by Paul A. Doyle

A comprehensive history of flying at this Hertfordshire location from 1912 to the present, detailing operational units, aircraft and building types. From its earliest beginnings as a World War One emergency landing ground, through the mid-war flying circus years, and on into the Second World War as an important Army Co-Operation airfield with Lysander, Mustang, Spitfire and Mosquito aircraft being some of the types operating from the site, this book gives all you wanted to find out about a site previously missed by researchers.

Plans show the development of the flying sites, layout and details of all buildings. Various appendices detail Commanding Officers, resident aircraft types, serials for resident aircraft along with their units, plus a full listing of all aerial incidents at or near the airfield.

96 pp, A4 size, softback, laminated cover, illustrated with 40 black and white photographs plus many maps and drawings.

£13.00 (by post in UK)

Please use reference ISBN 0 9525624 0 5 when ordering through booksellers